9788171094783

A TIME FOR HEALING

GUIDEBOOK FOR INNER HEALING RETREATS

By

Sr. Mary Usha S.N.D

A Time For Healing

This is Sister Mary Usha's second book on Inner Healing. The first book "Hidden Springs TO Healing" was published in 1984 and has found an eager reading public, both in India and abroad.

In my foreword I wrote at that time:

"The application of the healing gifts of the Holy Spirit to simple psychology seems very significant. Grace builds on nature: grace also transforms nature and often transcends nature's limitations. It is to Sister Mary Usha's credit that she has pioneered in this field. It is our hope that many will join in developing the ministry of inner healing through prayerful discernment and for the sake of those who suffer."

(August 1st, 1984).

This hope has been fulfilled: many have begun to pray with people for a deeper peace and healing of hurtful memories. Sister Mary Usha's ministry too has grown and expanded to the point where at present as member of the N.S.T. she is full-time engaged in giving Inner Healing Retreats, for which there is a great demand.

In this second book "A Time To Heal", Sister Mary Usha shares her Inner Healing Retreats in great detail. The text is laid out as an Eight Days' Retreat, with the customary Retreat Exercises (Morning Prayer, Meditation, Holy Hour, Eucharist) built round the framework of three "Common Reflections" (which are teaching and learning sessions) and a common sharing at night.

The topics for the Common Reflections are generally familiar to Retreat Preachers, but each is placed in the context of some aspect of Inner Healing.

This book "A Time To Heal" is a very useful tool and resource book for Retreat Preachers, who can use it to communicate the Healing Love of Jesus more fully to the many who suffer inwardly.

It can also be used for an 8 days' Retreat made privately, or with one or more companions. May it help make Inner Healing the experience of every one in the Church and beyond.

Aug. 20th, 1992 *Father Jim Borst, MHM*

A TIME FOR HEALING

There is a season for everything
A time for every occupation under heaven
A time for giving birth
A time for dying
A time for planting
A time for uprooting what has been planted
A time for killing
A time for healing
(Qoheleth / Ecclesiastes 3:1-3)

You are to tell them, "Yehweh says this:
If someone falls, can he not stand up again?
If people stray, can they not turn back?
. . . Even the stork in the sky knows the appropriate season;
turtledove, swallow and crane observe their time of migration.
Jeremiah 8:4-7)

After John had been arrested, Jesus went into Galilee.
There he proclaimed the gospel from God saying,
"The time is fulfilled, and the kingdom of God is close at hand.
Repent, and believe the gospel." **(Mark 1:14-15)**

DEDICATION

This book is lovingly dedicated to my parents, Mr. and Mrs. Varghese Pattassery. On the occasion of their golden wedding anniversary I wish to offer this gift as a small sign of my affection for them. I thank God for my parents, and for all other faithful mothers and fathers like them, whose self- sacrificing love reflects the divine life so beautifully. May God bless all families abundantly !

SPECIAL THANKS

To all those who have invited me over the past ten years to conduct Inner Healing Retreats, my gratitude. Thanks also to those who have taken notes during retreats and have typed them so that I might be able to put together this book. Among these hardworking associates special appreciation to Fr. Franklin Lobo, Mr. Anthony Lobo, Bertie and Conny Hyde and Mary Louise Samuel. To many enthusiastic participants who have made IHRs in Bombay, Goa, Bangalore, Madras, Calcutta, Bangladesh and Patna. My special gratitude to Frs. Fio Mascarenhas, Rufus Pereire and Gino Henrigues for inviting me every year to Bombay's Bible College for sessions with the students, whose attention and determination to make good use of healing skills energised me to write this set of guidelines for many others like them on fire with God's love and zeal to be of service for divine healing. To Frs. Jim Borst, Fio and Varkey Perekkatt who In the early days of the movement recognised the gift of healing in me and gently nudged me to get involved in the retreat ministry. To India's National Charismatic Service Team, of which I am a member; my on-going relationship with this community is a source of constant strength and growth for me. To Nisha, S.N.D., my own sister and close friend; finally, to my provincial, Sr. M. Shobana, S.N.D. for continually supporting me in too many ways to list here.

TABLE OF CONTENTS

PART			PAGE
INTRODUCTION			5
DAY ONE	:	TRUSTING	24
DAY TWO	:	LISTENING	49
DAY THREE	:	WONDERING	77
DAY FOUR	:	REMEMBERING	92
DAY FIVE	:	TURNING	110
DAY SIX	:	FORGIVING	137
DAY SEVEN	:	THANKING	148
DAY EIGHT	:	FOLLOWING	161
APPENDIX A	:	POINTS FOR OPTIONAL DAYS	180
DAY NINE	:	REACHING OUT	180
DAY TEN	:	GROWING	180
APPENDIX B	:	THE JOHARI WINDOW	189
APPENDIX C	:	CATCHING DREAMS	193

INTRODUCTION

Peter said, " I have neither silver nor gold, but I will give you what I have: in the name of Jesus Christ the Nazarene, walk!" Then Peter took the cripple man by the right hand and helped him to stand up. Instantly his feet and ankles became firm, he jumped up, stood, and began to walk, and he went with Peter and John into the temple, walking and jumping and praising God. (Ac. 3:6-8)

This short passage of sacred scripture challenges me constantly. It challenges my personal faith in Jesus Christ as living Lord and active Healer. This word stands also as a symbol and summary of what is happening in many places today throughout India and many other countries. Whether they realise it or not, the world's poor and cripple are inviting Christ's disciples to be channels of his divine healing for them.

Wherever I go, I see the poor. Their poverty is not just a matter of money. The poor as I understand and use the word here are those who do not have the bare necessities in order to live and grow as human beings. The poor also include those who do not possess the physical, mental, emotional and spiritual essentials. Yes, these too are truly crippled, truly poor. Some call them the destitute. They may not know exactly why they have to struggle so hard each day to keep themselves and their families alive. They may not even be aware that living as human beings can be any different from what they now experience as life-on-earth. But the poor know they're hurting. They know that, if they are to survive and to grow, they need help from others. So, they reach out--with their hands, their eyes, their just being there as they are. Yes, for every poor who raises her/his voice, there is another who has gone silent and hopeless. They don't believe anyone cares about them. They've given up thinking that life can change, that the daily pain will go away.

Now all this, which I've just said, is not new. It is not a new thing that tens of millions of hopeful and hopeless poor in India--and indeed in every land--today challenge believers to look at and to really see them, to draw near, to talk with them with human concern, and finally to pronounce that healing word in the power of God's name. What is new in our day is that more and more christian disciples are calling upon Christ in faith to put right our wounded world. Christians are beginning to think globally and to heal locally. We're seeing the Acts of the Apostles lived again as we prepare to celebrate the third millenial anniversary of Jesus' coming into our midst as fellow- pilgrim and Saviour. God's Spirit is preparing a marvellous birthday gift for this coming event.

Our age has been called a "privileged season of the Holy Spirit." We're living in A TIME FOR HEALING. Encouraged by God's Spirit, our world's simple, hurting, vulnerable poor are crying out. And the Lord's family members are bidden by his Spirit to answer. Let me give a few simple examples of what I mean.

Healing In A Crowded Train Compartment

Some time ago I was travelling on the Calcutta-Delhi Express. Anyone who has been in a second class railway compartment in north India knows the pattern. Getting into the over-crowded compartment, there is the normal excitement-sometimes utter confusion. You find your seat and settle down. Once the train begins to move, there are sighs of relief. Then a fascinating group dynamics among passengers begins. Newspapers and magazines are quietly exchanged with people who were, until a few minutes before, perfect strangers. If a family is travelling and it's meal time, often members will offer a share of food and water with other passengers. Initial fears and anxieties of travelling begin to give way to relaxation and celebration of life as though everyone were next door neighbours.

The person sitting beside me noticed my religious garb. Thinking that I was some sort of medical person, he told me that he had a bad headache. From his clothes and manner of speaking I could make out that he wasn't well-to-do or much educated. I had with me neither medicine nor extra money to buy something to ease this patient's aching head. From my inner healing ministry, however, I was familiar with common root causes for many headaches. So, when he expressed his need for relief, I became at once aware within me that I had something much more valuable for him than temporary quick-fix pills. I prayed to the Lord, that His Spirit would give me the right words to say. Then I enquired of this man if, by chance, anyone had hurt him recently. He looked at me for a moment in silent thought, as if to discover what being hurt by someone had to do with his headache. Then he said that, in fact, there was somebody who had injured him. I asked whether he was ready to forgive that person without judging his motives or intentions. The patient shook his head, indicating to me that he was ready for reconciliation. In a soft voice, audible only to this man and myself, I prayed to Jesus that He touch him with His love. I then thanked the Lord together with my brother here that He was now reconciling him and his neighbour who had offended him. Finally, I asked the Lord to heal him of his headache. This whole transaction had taken only a few minutes. By the end of it my travelling companion told me that the headache was gone. It had vanished! He added: "Why don't you tell me more about this Jesus? And I gladly did.

Helping A Distressed Lady In A Bus

Another example. This time in a Bihar State Transport bus, which was on its way from the capital, Patna, to a small town in central Bihar. I found myself seated next to a middle-aged lady who was having a breathing problem. Agitated and in obvious distress, she glanced towards me, fixing her eyes upon the crucifix around my neck. She told me she was having difficulty in breathing and requested me to help her. I informed her in Hindi that I was not a doctor or nurse, but that if she wished I would pray to the Lord Jesus for her. Her immediate question then was typical of many non-christians whom I have met while travelling: "If I myself pray to Jesus, will He listen *even to me?*" I smiled and assured her that Jesus loves everyone and listens to anyone who calls upon Him for help. The result of the prayer I offered with her audibly was that her breathing became normal and she was able to travel the rest of her journey comfortably.

I could relate other incidents much like these, which I and people I know have had, but let these two suffice to point out a curious fact. It is this: when wealthy people, who have much academic education, hear accounts like these experiences, their reaction is often one of disbelief. "This sounds like magic!" "It's not all that simple," they tell me. But poor people have no difficulty at all understanding that little miracles like these happen. The poor are, moreover, delighted to hear that Jesus loves them and heals them. Poor people are quick to believe and to claim such healing for themselves and their loved ones.

No One To Go To But You, Lord

Upon some reflection, it's not so strange after all. The poor cannot disguise their many wounds. They don't know how. Nor do they have the facilities to do so. The rich can and do relieve themselves rather easily from many common aches and pains by use of powerful--and expensive--new drugs. For their deeper sicknesses and human miseries attached to being mortal, wealthy folks can distract themselves with costly addictions. They sometimes speak and act as though they had no real need of any Higher Power than that which they purchase, when needed. They are also able to cover up their own and their family tragedies-- as though it were a stigma to be sick, to be suffering from an hereditary mental sickness or physical handicap. How many rich Indian children suffering from inherited physical and mental illnesses live and die in almost total isolation because they are looked upon as objects of family shame!

Today's Poor Bring People To God

Mother Teresa of Calcutta's slums claims that these days the world's poor are bringing people to God. This is true. When the apostle Peter was asked by the Lord whether he also wanted to abandon Him along with the other disgruntled disciples, that poor

INTRODUCTION

fisherman answered, "Lord, to whom shall we go?" (Jn. 6:68) Peter's faith is that of the simple, deep faith of the poor. They know they must open themselves to the Lord's healing in order to live and be saved. They also come quickly to know that they can become instruments of Christ's transforming touch. Again, this isn't new in the 1990's. What is new is the amount of healing that is going on all around us. The poor happily are "wounded healers", like Jesus Himself was. The poor intuitively understand Him and He them. It's not surprising that St. Francis of Assisi, who is called "the little poor man", composed this prayer of healing.

O Lord, make of me an instrument of Thy peace:
Where there is hatred, let me put love,
Where there is resentment, let me put forgiveness,
Where there is discord, let me put unity,
Where there is doubt, let me put faith,
Where there is error, let me put truth,
Where there is despair, let me bring happiness,
Where there is sadness, let me bring joy,
Where there is darkness, let me bring light.

O Master, grant that I may desire rather:
To console, than to be consoled,
To understand, rather than to be understood,
To love, rather than to be loved.

Because it is:
In giving, that we receive,
In forgiving, that we obtain forgiveness,
In dying, that we rise to eternal life.

A TIME FOR HEALING

This is a favourite prayer not only of Mother Teresa but of countless other people of all faiths. Francis takes inspiration for this beautiful prayer from his Guru and Lord, Jesus. Francis found this revelation in Christ's sermon on the mount. as it is proclaimed in St. Luke's "gospel of the poor".

How blessed are you who are poor:
The Kingdom of God is yours.
Blessed are you who are hungry now:
You shall have your fill.
Blessed are you who are weeping now:
You shall laugh.
Blessed are you when people hate you,
drive you out, abuse you,
denounce your name as criminal,
on account of the Son of man,
Rejoice when that day comes and dance for joy !
Look ! Your reward will be great in heaven.
This was the way their ancestors treated the prophets.

(Lk. 6:20-23)

A TIME FOR HEALING is my grateful response to the poor of India, for their friendship and for the welcome given by them to my first volume, *Hidden Springs To Healing*. One reader of that small work, who has suffered long years from the disease of alcoholism, wrote me these words:

I usually don't read books. But this book is special, because it touched my heart. Books of this sort help humanity. Because it has touched my heart, I have hope to continue my life. This is the kind of book we should encourge others to write.

INTRODUCTION

Needless to say, when a writer receives even a single letter like this, all the pains of writing are forgotten and transformed into joyful thanks; for, a priceless human being has been born to life!

I wish here to point out the close connection: (1) between *A Time For Healing* and my earlier book, *Hidden Springs To Healing*, and (2) between inner healing retreats and charismatic retreats, as they are conducted at present in India. Practically all those witnesses whose accounts appear in *Hidden Springs To Healing* had taken part in one or more inner healing retreats. *Springs* was written to help participants of both kinds of retreats. Let me describe briefly the relationship between these two different healing experiences, as I understand them.

Inner Healing And Charismatic Retreats

When people come to make an inner healing retreat (IHR), I do *not* expect them to have already made a charismatic retreat (CR). Some people have, many have not. Ideally, the preferred order is for them to make first an IHR. Why? The reasons are clear. Usually a CR has very many participants often in the hundreds and the staff is always pressed for opportunity in order to give each person even an hour's time. Within this short duration retreatants do well if they become aware of one or two inner blocks and be able to get the help needed for basic healing. I think this is why we see so many participants of CRs returning each year for another retreat. Healing is a *process*, a faith- pilgrimage from the womb-to-the-tomb. Only by *unhurried* stages each peron comes to discover one wounded relationship after another, so that each may be surrendered to the Lord for healing. Here again we see the divine loving-kindness at work as God reveals to us our multiple brokenness *little-by-little*. In this way we can more easily cope with the painful reality of our own woundedness, rather than be overwhelmed by it were God to reveal to us all at once the total extent of our weakness and needs. In the light of this, as St. Therese of Lisieux puts it, we can become willing to bear serenely the trial of being displeasing to ourselves.

11

The organisation of IHRs is different. Participant numbers are much smaller at most 40 and every retretant is, in fact, part of the healing team. An IHR is very much a do-it-together project. While there is plenty of time for individual prayer and solitude with the Lord, every day there are several periods for individual and small group inner healing sessions. The Lord is most generous in answering these petitions. Nor should anyone be surprised at this. In very clear terms He has promised us to expect His generous response when our needs are expressed to Him, especially through a prayerful community:

> *In truth I tell you once again, if two of you on earth agree to ask anything at all it will be granted to you by my Father in heaven. For where two or three meet in my name, I am there among them* (Mt. 18:19-20)

IHRs are a way of claiming in faith the healing we need. This is based upon trust in the Lord's own promise to be present and, therefore, healing whenever disciples gather together in His name.

One Lord Of All

While on this subject of praying in Jesus' sacred name, I wish to mention a request that came to me recently to publish a kind of religious non-denominational edition of my work. The reason given was this: a book which is not explicitly Christian will appeal to a much wider reading public here in India. I think the suggestion is made with a good intention. It also takes into consideration our country's situation of being culturally pluriform, the cradle for many great religious traditions. Concretely, what is suggested to me is that instead of using exclusively the name "Jesus", the term "Lord" be employed. In response to this suggestion let me say I realise that relatively very few people in India will ever have an opportunity to experience an IHR. Of those who do, all will be members of the Christain community, who make up about two percent of our sub-continent's more than 850 million population. On the other hand, thousands even, tens of thousands of my Hindu and Muslim sisters/brothers can with profit read about IHRs. If the basic mes-

INTRODUCTION

sage of healing can be received and welcomed by those of other faiths through use of Christ's sacred title "Lord", then I am it. I utterly believe there is but one God of all human beings. This wonderful God, Lord and Advocate Father, Son, and Spirit abides actively in all people. God accepts with love all sacred names which we reverently use in prayer to acknowledge the gifts of creation, redemption and sanctification. So, besides my original, explicitly christian edition, I am also happy that other vernacular translations use the title "Lord" in order that many followers of other esteemed religions may read, understand and identify with the good news message of healing and salvation for them. This means that by a non - denominational edition more people can become aware that there are marvels of healing and deliverance being worked for all God's children-- whosoever call upon Him as Lord and Saviour (see Ac 10:34-35). In this context I remember that one day His disciples came to Jesus complaining that someone not of their community was healing people by using his name. The exclusive and intolerant disciples tried to stop him. Jesus' response is heartening for India: "You must not stop him; no one who works a miracle in my name could soon afterwards speak evil of me. Anyone who is not against us is for us." (Mk 9:39-40)

Short History Of Inner Healing Retreats

As my memories go back to the origin of IHRs in India, at once I recall the very happy years I spent teaching children at pre- school level. These two ministries Montesorri teaching and involvement in IHRs are closely connected for me. An image of Jesus embracing toddlers often flashes vividly to my mind. The gospel scene of St. Mark says so much between the lines. The Lord's disciples were scolding some mothers who wanted Jesus just to touch their babies and pray for them. When Jesus saw that these poor mothers were being driven away, he was indignant.

> "Let the little children come to me; do not stop them; for it is to such as these that the kingdom of God belongs. In truth I tell you, anyone who does not welcome the kingdom of God like a little child will never enter it."

A TIME FOR HEALING

> *Then Jesus embraced them. laid his hands on them and gave them his blessing.* (Mk. 10:14-16)

Strange as it may seem, what is today known as inner healing retreats really began in my Montessori classes ! Day after day I beheld the painful, bewildering confusion of these little *kids,* ages three to five. As a gift of God I have always been very sensitive towards little ones and their many changes of moods. Very early in my teaching career I realised that youngsters' behaviour unconsciously but accurately reflects their own home situations, like mirrors. Seeing their suffering each day in Montessori class I wanted to help my tiny friends to find peace, so they could enjoy their classes and their lives. It was at once clear to me, however, that the key to helping these babies was to enter into the lives of their disturbed parents. Without counselling skills I couldn't do this. Thus it was that after ten years of montessori teaching, in 1975 I went to Vellore's Christian Counselling Centre to learn how I could better help my students and their parents.

This time in Vellore was an enriching experience for me. the counselling programme was very practical, combining theory with actual practice. Several times a week we student counsellors were sent to the nearby Christian Medical College Hospital to interview patients. I learned very much from these contacts. In particular I began to realise: (1) the marvellous inter connection of body, mind, spirit, and (2) the effects of our unconscious and subconscious past upon present behaviour.

At the end of that same year another important event for my future ministry took place. At Patna's regional pastoral centre, Navjyoti Niketan, I had my first experience of charismatic retreats both as a participant and also as an unofficial staff. Fresh and enthusiastic from my Vellore training, I found myself from day one of this retreat praying with other retreatants for healing of wounded memories and broken relationships. This doesn't mean that I was busy with everyone except myself! On the contrary, during those eight days I experienced God deeply and powerfully. One of the animating team members, Fr Jim Borst, MHM, recognised that the Lord had given me healing gifts; he encouraged me to volunteer for the

INTRODUCTION

retreat ministry. Because of my Montessori and Vellore preparation, I was enabled to interpret this suggestion as a sign of divine guidance. It didn't seem to me to be from pride or presumption. Rather, this invitation to enter the healing ministry seemed to me a call from the Lord for which I had been prepared step-by-step-. I was further strengthened in this judgment by scriptural passages that providentially caught my attention with new force and meaning. Like the following:

> *Each one of you has received a special grace, so, like good stewards responsible for all these varied graces of God, put it at the service of others. If anyone is a speaker, let it be as the words of God, if anyone serves, let it be as in strength granted by God' so that in everything God may receive the glory, through Jesus Christ, since to him alone belong all glory and power for ever and ever. Amen. (1 P 4:9-11)*

'So, the following year in late December, 1976, at Navjyoti, I joined the charismatic team for the first time as a full-fledged staff memeber. I made myself fully available throughout the retreat to pray with people for inner healing. After that event, the Lord arranged more than enough work for me. And fifteen years later I'm still busy!

IHRs At The National Level

In 1977 I received a green light from my Notre Dame Congregation to work full-time in the inner healing ministry. In 1978 I became a member both of India's charismatic retreat ministry's National Service team and its National Advisory Council. That same year Bombay hosted the national charismatic convention. There were three days of convention and an additional three days devoted to physical healing sessions. For the entire six days from early morning to late at night I was occupied with one-to- one encounters for inner healing. To my knowledge, this was the first time in India that full-time inner healing services were offered to people at the national level. That convention was also particularly memorable for another reason. An international charismatic team had come to Bombay to be part of the core staff. Each of these experts showed real interest to learn how I went about my inner healing work. This meant much to me by way of confirmation to move ahead in my new apostolate. The encouragement came at a time I needed it and I'm grateful to those sisters and brothers who were channels for me of the Lord's gentle guidance.

Extending IHRs To Large Parishes in Regional Languages

Over a period of two weeks in 1979 I began a fruitful relationship with the Bible College in Bomaby. For the next seven years this appointment became an annual event. I found deep satisfaction both in helping such mature, intelligent bible students with their own inner healing processes and animating them to become agents of inner healing for others. That same year Mr. Anthony Lobo and his priest brother, Franklin Lobo, CSSR, invited me to give my first Inner Healing Retreat. It was arranged at Our Lady of Salvation Church, Dadar, Bombay, where Monsignor Jonathan Dias hosted two hundred retreatants for five days. Immediately after this retreat I teamed up with Anthony and Fr. James D'Souza in Bombay and together we conducted city-wide inner healing retreats at the Bandra Retreat House. Each was of five days with about one hundred retreatants, most of whom were laity. Up to this time IHRs had been conducted exclusively in English. In 1980-81 at Bassein, however, I conducted a series of 4-5 days' IHRs in Hindi, with simulataneous translation into Marathi. With my limited command of Hindi this was a difficult challenge for me, because it meant creating a new vocabulary in various regional languages. I realise that much more reflection and research needs to be done in order to be accurate and effective when IHRs are conducted in languages other than English. Collaboration on the regional level is needed, a team of people skilled in various disciplines.

IHRs Internationally

Today, ten years later, the number of Indian cities which have had IHRs has grown fast. Looking back over the decade, I see that the Lord has arranged all things with a timeliness and gentle power that leaves me in wonderment. The Lord has also made it possible for me to extend these services internationally, by conducting retreats in Bangla Desh, Italy and France. Yes, I pray in tongues but no, I am not a polyglot! During every second of my international retreats, translators like assisting angels stood by my side translating into their own language what I spoke in my own simple English. How these retreats were arranged abroad would fill a chapter in itself. All I need say now, with full conviction, is that the way IHRS began and the way they have spread throughout India and into other countries is God's arranging, not mine. I have always felt myself as a small, fragile paint brush in the hand of a master artist. I'm very thrilled that the Lord uses me; the credit for the beautiful, lasting results goes to the Lord. I state this not out of some sort of routine ritual of humility. It is my permanent inner attitude towards this ministry. During every inner healing retreat I strive to focus my eyes and heart on Jesus continually- literally, night and day. He is the team Guide and Director. To put it more concretely, I keep one eye and ear on the Lord, the other eye and ear on the retreatants.

I turn now to the retreat dynamics, about which I wish to speak only briefly. The gist of what I say, though, is important and needs to be emphasised throughout the retreat.

The Dynamics Of An Inner Healing Retreat

Unlike charismatic retrats, IHRs do not have a set order of input reflections. The content and the pace of an IHR come mainly from the retreatants' *specific needs.* This important principle needs to be stressed from the very beginning because not a few retreatants--particularly religious and priests--are used to clear-cut, detailed structures. Typically they are uncomfortable with non-structured programme. This apparent absence of direction in an IHR makes it more like a play-it-by-ear workshop than a retreat with its characteristic, set patterns.

A TIME FOR HEALING

In an IHR there are no prearranged "talks". Content, priorities and order of topics are determined from listening closely to the retreatants, sharing. This is constantly analyzed by the staff with the retreatants, so that over an eight or ten days' period the classical phases of any retreat do emerge. First come the days of purgation, then of illumination, followed by those of communion. Since there is no pre-arrangement of material there has to be throughout discernment of spirits. (The international charismatic service's book on discernment by Fr Fio Mascarenhas, S.J. is helpful for those unfamiliar with this essential spiritual skill.) To carry on such discernment everyday there must be a staff meeting usually the last thing at night. At this important session the team prays first, giving thanks for the day's graces. This is followed by an informal but forthright evaluation of what is happening within the retreat community- retreatants and staff. On the basis of this data a plan is made for the following day's liturgy and general orientation. The core group session ends with another thanksgiving prayer.

How fast and at what depth the group moves depends upon the participants. Responsibility for a fruitful retreat is with every retreatant individually and with the group as a community. The number of sharing sessions each day puts heavy emphasis on the retreatants' responsibility to participate actively and openly.

Key Points For An Introductory Talk

As the IHR begins there are four general directives that need to be mentioned emphatically.

(1) CONFIDENTIALITY : Because there is much personal sharing, both team members and retreatants maintain a rule of secrecy. What is shared and observed within the group may not be revealed to others outside the group. Some therapeutic groups put a sign up for all to read and obey, like the following: *"WHAT YOU SEE HERE, WHAT YOU HEAR HERE, WHEN YOU LEAVE HERE, LET IT STAY HERE!"*

INTRODUCTION

This holds both for positive and negative material. Mutual trust is more easily and quickly built up, if everyone feels confident that whatever is talked about stays within the retreat community.

(2) PARTICIPANTS ARE PAIRED OFF BY THE STAFF : For some retreat exercises, participants are paired for prayer and sharing. The choice of partners is made by the team before hand. Some of the factors that are considered in deciding these sharing groups are:--(a) maturity/immaturity, (b) ethnic and sexual prejudices, both positive and negative, (c) likelihood of positive/negative transference. A word on this third criterion. When people start personal sharing with another individual or in a small group, consciously and unconsciously they start relating to strangers in the group on the basis of their past relationships, esp. those with parents and close relatives. This psychological mechanism of transference is for healing purposes promoted by skilled psychologists in order to "re-parent". This means the counsellor sees a need to modify a person's way of relating to significant others because of early unhealthy relationships, particularly between the child and its parents. In IHRs staff members are aware of the possibility of transference, but they do not promote it--being beyond both their competence and the limitations of time. During a retreat the focus is on Christ, the Healer, present in the group as He was with the two disciples travelling to Emmaus (see Lk. 24:13-35). For its part, the group expresses acceptance of each person in a number of ways--by attentive listening to them, by praying for them daily, and in healing sessions by respectfully placing hands on their heads and interceding for them.

(3) RETREAT READING : Much use of the Bible is encouraged throughout the retreat. As reconciliation and deep healing begins to take place, the Word of God becomes more and more alive for the participants. They are being opened up and watered by God's powerful love through the action of Christ's Holy Spirit. The parable of the seed sown in different kinds of soil challenges the retreatants to be open and generous (see Mt 13:4- 9, 18-23). Great biblical personalities -- Joseph in Egypt, Saul, David, Sarah and Hagar,

A TIME FOR HEALING

Moses, Elizabeth, John the Baptist, Zacchaeus, Martha and Mary, Peter--are looked at with new understanding and compassion, as being fellow pilgrims who also struggled with broken relationships and the burden of wounded memories as we ourselves today. *Hidden Springs To Healing* is recommended to help retreatants see that the way reconciliation is central to all healing and how, without it, life becomes disastrous.

(4) NOTE-TAKING: In IHRs retreatants are advised to keep personal records in the form of spiritual diaries. This kind of note-taking is indicated for a number of reasons. First of all, retreatants receive many insights into the mystery of their personalities and their key inter-personal relationships. They are encouraged to jot down these discoveries to make them <u>more coherent</u>. Secondly, most participants have to be introduced to new skills: like "catching dreams". Retreatants are taught to write down a short description of their dreams upon waking each day. Later they are helped to <u>interpret their symbolism in order to discover</u> how helpful dream-analysis can be for understanding themselves. Finally, the most <u>important motive for a personal diary during this kind of experience is to record inspirations from God.</u> For good reason some people like to call these "<u>anointed words</u>". Coming from sacred scriptures and other sources they are graces from the Lord to lighten the way not only during this time of healing but for the rest of their earthly pilgrimage. Long after the IHR, each person can read and re-read what they had jotted down. Thus the original experience can again and again be renewed and deepened.

Sample IHR Time-Table

The time-table given here is recommended for most groups. Of course this is open to adjustments called for by local conditions.

6:15 A.M. MORNING PRAYER : together in the chapel. Prayer of the Church is celebrated. With laity groups the psalms are read from the Bible.

INTRODUCTION

6:45 A.M. BREAKFAST : with recorded instrumental music played for maintaining a prayerful atmosphere.

7:30 A.M. MEDITATION : one full hour of personal prayer. The topic is suggested by a staff member according to the day's theme, but each retreatant is encouraged to follow the lead of the Spirit.

8:30 A.M. COMMON REFLECTION I : an animator guides the group in reflection upon some basic aspect of inner healing. There is much dialogue during this time, which is kept as informal as possible, striving to focus on the group's personal experiences. After an hour, small groups are assigned for that day's sharing and prayer.

10:15 A.M. FREE TIME

10:45 A.M. COMMON REFLECTION II : (as above)

12:00 P.M. LUNCH : with recorded music that is culturally acceptable to the group. Free time follows to allow for rest, relaxation & individual prayer--the way of the Cross and recitation of the rosary are left to each individual's devotion. During all free time the animating team offers one-to-one sessions for counselling and inner healing to those who so desire. A list is posted with each staff member's name and where she/he will be available to meet with the retreatants. They are then assigned a time with the staff member of their choice.

2:30 P.M. HOLY HOUR : this is an opportunity for adoration before the Blessed Sacrament exposed.

3:30 P.M. TEA

4:00 P.M. COMMON REFLECTION III : (as above)

6:00 P.M. EUCHARISTIC CELEBRATION : as far as possible, the assigned readings of the day are followed. When options are allowed, readings are chosen thematically to harmonise with the retreat's topic for that particular day.

7:00 P.M. SUPPER: with recorded music.

8:00 P.M. NIGHT COMMON SHARING: this is a period devoted to retreatants' evaluation of the whole day. Reviewing the 24 hour journey, retreatants recall how they spent their time, what graces they received and what difficulties they experienced.

9:00 P.M. TEAM EVALUATION: time for staff prayer, review, discernment, planning and thanksgiving for all the helps and hindrances met with during that day of pilgrimage with the Lord and his disciples.

Acknowledgements

A final introductory note has to do with a pleasant duty of acknowledging much help given me to make this small book possible.

(a) Biblical citations have been taken from THE NEW JERUSALEM BIBLE.

(b) Quotations of Vatican II are from Austin Flannery's 1988 Revised Edition. Wherever necessary inclusive language is used, being careful to express exactly the original meaning.

(c) Many persons have contributed to the contents of A TIME FOR HEALING. Wherever I have presented stories of an autobiographical nature, I have changed the authors' names and incidental details in order to protect confidenitality. Lastly, while taking full responsibility for everything in this book, I need to say in truth that this book is a *community project*. Only the Lord can give adequate thanks to all those who have contributed to its making.

INTRODUCTION

To nurture us, to bring the best out of us, God has sent many people into our lives--parents, relatives, friends, teachers, acquaintances. They have guided us the way they knew, and we have become what we are today thanks to them. How much of our true, God-given talents and potentical have we used to serve the Lord and humanity: 10%? 20%? 50%? And what of our unused power, which God has given so generously but which we so miserly have not used? It is like that barren land, that field covered with useless weeds and wild growth described in Jeremaiah 4:3. Today the Lord confronts each one of us as He confronted the people of ancient Israel, *"I had planted you, a red vine of completely sound stock. How is it you have turned into seedlings of a vine that is alien to me?"* (Jr 2:21) Negative feelings and emotions are like poisonous plants that keep us from using our total potential. They choke life and gradually extend themselves into more and more of our lives. The Lord says, *"Now is the real time of favour. Now is the time for healing. Now is the day of salvation!"*

DAY ONE

A TIME FOR HEALING: BY TRUSTING

If you...evil as you are, know how to give your children what is good, how much more will the heavenly Father give the Holy Spirit to those who ask him. (Lk 11:13)

*AIM OF THE DAY : To discover how better (a) to pray in the Spirit; (b) to trust Him and others; (c) to invest in this new community of retreatants, whom the Father has given us as companions for retreat days of our pilgrimage to Him.

* MORNING PRAYER : Psalm 42-43 *("As a deer yearns for running streams...").* During this retreat we want God to teach us how to pray more personally, more deeply. Each day we choose a theme which indicates the spirit of the day's reflection and in a way summarises the grace we ask. The theme text for Day One, given above from Luke's eleventh chapter, is within a setting of three teachings on prayer. Jesus' disciples are watching Him at prayer. Respectfully they wait until He finishes and then make that beautiful request, which we wish today to make our own, *"Lord, teach us to pray..."* Jesus teaches us today just as He instructed His disciples to *ask, search, knock, persist* in our supreme quest of the Father's gift-of-gifts, the Holy Spirit. The Spirit is the only teacher of authentic prayer.

During this retreat we begin our day by focusing on the psalms rightly called Christ's own prayer book. Praying over these ancient songs each morning we join the whole Church around the world in a liturgy of praise and petition. We unite ourselves with Jesus and His Body, His Pilgrim Priestly People. Today's selection, Ps 42-43, was originally the individual lament of an exiled levite, a person consecrated to God, yearning for an experience of the divine presence. Our method of celebrating this Prayer Of The Church is

DAY ONE : TRUSTING

to recite the psalm slowly, alternating between two groups, as in a choral recitation. After completing each psalm, we pause for silent reflection, to allow the Lord to speak to us more deeply. These are words inspired by God's Spirit. We are aware that their message needs to be completed with the fullness of Christ's revelation. But we also want to appreciate what Vatican II teaches about this and other books of the Old Testament:

> These books, even though they contain matters imperfect and provisional, nevertheless they show us authentic divine teaching. Christians should accept with veneration these writings. Which give expression to a lively sense of God, which are a storehouse of sublime teaching on God and of sound wisdom on human life, as well as a wonderful treasury of prayers; in them, too, the mystery of salvation is present in a hidden way.

(Dogmatic Constitution On Divine Revelation, 15)

After a period of silent reflection upon the sacred text, the animator invites participants to repeat phrases or words of the psalms which touch them. They are requested to share briefly the reason why the selected words are meaningful to them this morning. With such an atmosphere of respectful attention and love, people find it easy to express their thoughts, feelings, and their faith along with their yearning to grow-in-the-Spirit.

* MEDITATION : This is for one hour of private prayer each day. The place of prayer is left to each person's preference. On Day One, however, we spend meditation time together because we want to initiate those who have never meditated before into the art of mental prayer. We also wish to help all retreatants to *relax* in the Lord's presence. We use the word "relaxation" in the yogic sense, which is the exact opposite of taking a lounging or lazy posture. To relax during prayer means to breathe easily and deeply, assuming a bodily posture in which there is no muscular strain. Our mind-body-spirit is alert, without tension. We focus pleasantly on a single

A TIME FOR HEALING

point: the Lord who is present. For about the first five minutes we simply breathe deeply. It also helps to close our eyes, partially at least, so that only a small amount of light enters. We become aware that Jesus, our Master and Friend, is with us and attentive to us. As we inhale slowly, deliberately, we fill up the lower parts of our lungs also. We pray to Christ that along with this fresh, clean air, He may come into us more and more. As we exhale gently and consciously, we ask the Lord, our divine Healer, to expel from us all impurities --physical and spiritual. We alow our whole being to be pliant and in harmony with everything around us. The animator may in a tranquil tone of voice call attention to noises that stand out and may tend to distract us. Instead, we invite them people, animals, birds to join us as we sit serenely at our Lord's feet. The animator is aware that perhaps not a few of the retreatants are present physically but not yet fully with all their hearts. It is my experience that many retreatants have not been praying well because they have been often blocked emotionally. This morning Jesus compassionately looks upon each pilgrim sister and brother with great love. The invitation He gave to His apostles is offered now: *"Come away to some lonely place all by yourselves and rest for a while"*. (Mk 6:31) That's what this retreat is all about: an invitation of the Lord drawing us as friends into the seclusion of 8-10 days to taste and see how good God is to experience His sabbath rest, His *shaantee!* After these few introductory remarks and exercises of relaxing, the animator leaves the group to be alone in silent attendance upon Christ, for whom they yearn, hunger and thirst. *"Why so downcast, why all these sighs ? Hope in God ! I will praise him still, my Saviour, my God." (Ps 43,5)*

* **COMMON REFLECTION I :** (*Note:* let me make an important observation to the readers of this book. The material I present under each of the Common Reflections is much more than I--or any other Staff member can present in a single period. My purpose in offering such plentiful material has a double purpose : (a) to give retreat animators options and (b) to give enough illustrations so that retreatants who are unfamiliar with the topics being discussed may understand as easily as possible).

DAY ONE : TRUSTING

The animator invites everyone to jot down briefly their answers to a few, leading questions:

(1) What are your expectations of this retreat? Put negatively, looking to our fears and anxieties, during these days what do you want NOT TO HAPPEN ? And positively, what do you want TO HAPPEN? What do you want to receive and to gain during this retreat?

(2) What are your likes and dislikes about this place of retreat?

(3) How did you spend the hour of prayer, which we just completed together in the chapel?

After each person has written down his/her answers, he/she is asked to share them with the person sitting next to them to their right. About ten minutes is devoted to this sharing five minutes for each partner. Afterwards, the animator asks volunteers to tell the group their answers. A summary of these points is put on the blackboard, so that the group can get a sense of what each member expects from the retreat, their response to the surroundings, and how they experienced their first hour of meditation. *Note :* tho overall method of retreats for inner healing is to learn by first doing and then evaluating, i.e. to experience something and immediately reflect upon it together under skilled guidance. You may notice how the aim of the first day is promoted by this sharing exercise: learning trust by actually trusting another person and the whole group with "inside information" about our thoughts, feelings, hopes and fears. In this way we invest in our new community. We empower the group with knowledge of our intimate selves. This is risk- taking, because persons may misuse such information. But, precisely by taking this risk, trust engenders trust. Retreatants will receive this knowledge gratefully and use it constructively. This is a big step towards building a faith community. Among the many advantages of those who are in a good sharing group are the following.

(1) We are all involved with basically the same struggle to *"live by the truth and in love"* (Ep 4:15). Pilgrims need other individuals; and, as anyone who has been on a pilgrimage well

knows, they also *essentially* need the faith community, in order to move ahead in-the-Lord.

(2) As we reveal our weaknesses and failings honestly and respectfully, we build a strong community of freedom, confidence and joy. We become more and more conscious of two great realities, that we are all wounded sinners and that we have all been redeemed by Christ. Our lives are an on-going process of claiming His healing and liberating grace. Letting others know our strengths is good but showing others these "credentials" may sometimes result in putting up a wall of separation between us and them. Our strong points are only part of us. Each of us brings into the retreat a history. This life history is composed of not only successes but also of defeats, failures, weaknesses. Some of these may be serious, like a terminal cancer. Especially in this sensitive task of building confidence amongst members of a new community, when we let others in the group know that we, too, are in need of help, we thereby help create a healthy atmosphere of mutual concern, compassion and non-defensiveness.

Distractions

During our retreat we take all distractions seriously. We want to make the best use of them, tracing these prayer blocks back to their sources. If possible, we want to identify their root causes. During these days together we will attempt to analyse not only our night-dreams but also our day-dreams. We call them "Distractions". After each period of prayer we pay careful attention to these recurring diversions during meditation. They can call our attention to a fear, an anxiety, or a value that is operative in our lives but which has escaped our recognition. We will now learn that distractions remind us of unfinished business. They challenge us to put things in right order. Distractions can uncover large areas within us that are in urgent need of the Lord's healing touch. Let's take a look at an example from the gospel.

As she prepared her honoured visitors' meal, Martha was very distracted. The words of Jesus invite this anxious hostess to set

DAY ONE : TRUSTING

her priorities right, putting first things first. *"Martha, Martha, you worry and fret about so many things, and yet few are needed, indeed only one."* (Lk 10:41) Mary, her sister, had chosen to listen to God's Word; and the Lord pronounced this "the better part", not to be taken from her by distractions, fretting, or some otherwise good services. Each of us needs to discover the Martha-Mary inclinations within our hearts and lives. There is a time for working and a time for praying. During this retreat we are encouraged to utilise even our distractions by first becoming conscious of them. The scriptural command is *" for all things give thanks; this is the will of God for you in Christ Jesus."* (1 Th 5:18) In obedience to this word we can therefore *surrender* all distractions to the Lord for Him to look after, while we keep ourselves centred on Him and what He wants to tell us. Thus, meditation is being-present-before-the-Lord, looking at Him, listening to Him, responding to Him. As our daily concern come crowding noisily into our attention in the form of distractions, we bring each to our beloved Lord for safe-keeping and healing. Gratefully we do this, knowing He will look after them, while we spend the time allotted to us focussed on Him. It's like working in an office. People keep coming to us, interrupting our work. What do we do? We attend to each one's needs and then quietly return to our original work. This is what we do with distractions during prayer. We could hurriedly try to brush them away as we do with flying insects that bother us. Rather, we take a good look at them. They are part of us not some invader. We want to recognise ourselves in them; we desire to be healed through them. These first few days of retreat we are not surprised that quite many "outside" thoughts bubble up to the surface of our awareness whenever we enter seriously into prayer. In a way, each distraction is a messenger for us. There may be matters of reconciliation that need our attention. There can be thoughts that come from hurt pride, fears and anxieties about our work or loved ones. Whatever the origin of these distractions, we bring them to the Lord and identify them by name. We ask ourselves fearlessly, "What's really in back of this distraction? what's at the bottom of it, its motivation?" We then request Christ to touch each distraction at its root. We admit frankly, "This is me, Lord! In this distraction it's I who is crying out in need of You. Thanks, that I can be honest with myself and with You, that I can surrender myself and this preoccupation (fear, anxiety, lack of trust, etc.) to You. Touch me now, Lord! Say only the word and I shall be healed. Praise to You, Lord!"

To summarise: distractions can be and should be incorporated into our prayer. This incorporation of day-dreams into our prayer happens this way. (1) We first become aware of the distractions. (2) We then identify and name them by searching out their causes. (3) Finally, we consciously turn them over to the Lord with thanksgiving. On this first day of retreat I encourage all retreatants to work seriously at this, preferably jotting down in their retreat diaries how they deal with their distractions. We want to make "catching day dreams" one of our new skills and a matter of new habit. For, we shall pray in the power of Christ's Spirit more deeply and completely, when we have this positive, inclusive attitude towards all "distractions". I close this reflection with an anecdote from the life of St.Teresa of Avila. A Doctor of the Church and master of prayer, Teresa is one of the most attractive, down-to-earth women who ever lived. In her writings she admits to having a distraction in prayer one day over the design of her congregation's new dress. It was such a persistent digression and at the same time such an important matter for Teresa that she decided to bring the whole matter before the Lord, to consult Him and ask Him what He thought. Her "distraction" thus became part of her prayer.

* COMMON REFLECTION II : In this second session we want to reflect upon TRUST. Some of us may have had the experience of trusting another person but were bitterly disappointed when that trust was violated. During retreat we want and need to share personal matters with freedom and confidence. Each one of us is precious to the Lord. Each of us lives in God's heart, beautiful persons, as God created us in Christ. God intends that we reflect His glory and light uniquely. This is our vocation. Our God-given mission is to strive to become on earth who we are already in His heart. Negative feelings, attitudes and behaviour mar this beauty. By negative feelings we are, "put into the dark". We experience this darkness as a heavy burden, sometimes it feels unbearable. Our faces reflect this. From our countenance, especially our eyes,

DAY ONE : TRUSTING

friends notice when we are in a "dark mood". There are a couple of difficulties with these negative feelings and the moods that come with them. (1) We're often not conscious when we have them. (2) We don't know what to do about them. It helps to be aware that everyone has these episodes, some persons more often than others. Perhaps some of the retreatants experience darkness and heaviness as a more or less permanent state, or at least for long periods of time. IHRs are designed to come to grips with these recurring bouts of moodiness. The Lord wants us *to shine*. He commands us to let our lives shine forth so that people will see the light and give praise to our Father (Mt 5:16). After an IHR a husband, whose wife had made the retreat very successfully, exclaimed to me, "Sister, my wife is so much more beautiful after the retreat !" It was literally true. His wife's inner beauty really shone out as a result of what had happened during the days of healing prayer. She had learned to TRUST others, herself and God. The results could be seen in a striking new radiance on her face. This is so typical that one of the veteran staff members of IHRs jokingly suggested to me that we need to have two photographs of each retreatant, one taken immediately before the retreat and the other just after. Learned TRUST is the key to this phenomenon of lighting-up personalities.

Assigning Partners

At this point I ask each retreatant to write down on a slip of paper the names of two or three persons in the retreat group with whom they want to share, people they will also pray for and help by trusting them. After the slips are collected the animating staff makes up a list of sharing partners, using the criteria mentioned in the introduction.

Sharing My Own Pilgrimage Of Trust

Next, I share something of my own growth in trust. A favourite passage for me is the incident in which Jesus is shown speaking to the fruitless, deceptive fig tree, that at once withers up. He then says to the disciples:

> *In truth I tell you, if you have faith and do not doubt at all, not only will you do what I have done to the fig tree, but even if you say to this mountain, "Be pulled up and thrown into the sea", it will be done. And if you have faith, everything you ask for in prayer, you will receive.* (Mt 21:21-22)

I can remember one day when I was challenged very strongly whether I really trusted God, whether I had this kind of faith-without-any-doubt. I decided then and there to pray to Christ's Holy Spirit for such a trust. Since that day I have learned how to pray to the Father for certain graces. When these prayers are answered, my faith seems like doubled. The Spirit has been teaching me this way of praying, step by step. Faith and action based upon that faith must go together. This is my understanding of the phrase, "Standing on the promises of the Lord." Some examples from my own life.

A Tourist Sent By The Lord

(1) A couple of years ago I was in a very remote area of Bihar. My ministry was almost fully devoted to conducting retreats for people living in villages. The daily schedule had to be adapted to that of the villagers' programme. They were so poor, that if they did not work, they did not eat. So there were whole seasons of the year when they were so occupied with planting or harvesting that I had heaps of leisure time. At the time of the following incident I had some free time because everyone around was engaged in cutting the crops. Whether it was part of being lonely for the people or what, I don't know but one day I experienced a deep desire to speak to others about how good God is. I remember praying, "Lord, bring me someone so that I may talk to them about You!" It was that simple. Two days later five foreign tourists showed up at our convent. Over a cup of tea at table, one of them turned to me and remarked that someone had told him that I conducted charismatic retreats. This person turned out to be a friend of a priest in our area. The tourist explained that in his native Australia many young people were interested in such retreats but that for older folks they were still something of a threat. He wanted me to share my views and how I had become involved in them. As he spoke, it was just

as though a voice said to me, "Now, Usha, this is your chance to tell someone about Me." Here was the answer to my prayer of 48 hours before? We talked for quite a while. I gave him a few booklets about the charismatic renewal in India and other countries. We also prayed together for the gift of discernment, asking the Lord to guide us to the places He wanted us to go and to the persons to whom He wished to send us. As I said goodbye to this traveller and his companions, I was also thanking the Lord for the way He had directed this stranger to me, thousands of kilometres from his home. As a result of this meeting my reliance upon God and prayer increased.

An Impossible Journey Made Easy

(2) About fifteen years ago, when I had just begun to get involved in IHRs but was still full-time in charge of our Montessori School in Patna, I received a telegram urgently requesting me to be in Bangalore within 72 hours in order to help out in a large retreat. I thought that this was practically speaking an impossible request. For, though it took three days to reach Bangalore with the best of connections, it required weeks, sometimes months, to get a train reservation, particularly at this time of school vacation. Anyway, I brought the message to my superior. She read it, looked at me in silence and shrugged her shoulders. This is exactly how I felt about it, too it was, under the circumstances, an unthinkable proposal, an "operation impossible". So, I went back to my work of checking report cards, which had to be distributed before closing our school for summer holidays. A few hours later at lunch a special announcement was made that an elderly member of our community had to be flown at once to Bangalore because of a serious health condition. A volunteer was needed to go along with her. Everyone was busy with examination corrections. Normally I was slow in preparing my reports, but for some inexplicable reason I had been able to complete my work early. To make a long story short, I became the travelling companion, arriving in Bangalore not only on time to begin the retreat but rested and with 24 hours to spare! What had seemed to me at first sight like an impossible journey turned out to be very comfortable.

Trusting God For What To Wear

(3) It was the winter of 1979. I travelled from Patna to Bombay to give a retreat to lay leaders. Since it was very cold in Bihar at that time, and not realising the big difference of weather in western India, I brought only warm clothes with me. One day during my retreat I was perspiring and near to suffocating from my heavy clothing. Towards evening I remember praying frantically, "Lord, You've got to provide me with some lighter clothes ! Otherwise, I won't be able to do your work. One more day like today and I think I'll collapse." Early next morning, while I was praying in the chapel before breakfast, one of the retreatants came asking if I could go with her just then to pray over her very sick mother. She lived nearby and it would take only a few minutes. I looked at my watch and saw that we had plenty of time; so, off we went. It had rained during the night and the street had large puddles of dirty water. As we waited for the traffic at a busy intersection, suddenly a truck sped by splashing sheets of water and leaving our dresses filthy from the gutter drainage. The whole thing happened so quickly that we could only look at each other dumbfounded. But inside me my quick reaction was to complain to the Lord, "Here we are doing your work, and see what You let happen to us!" Recovering some of my peace, I was able to relieve the young women of her embarassment at all this trouble by saying that everything would be OK because the Lord knows what He's doing. "Come on," I said forcing a smile, "even though we don't understand the reasons, we're going to give this accident to Him *with thanks !*" We even managed to laugh a little over our "ridiculous" gratitude. When we reached her home, my companion gave me one of her mother's light cotton dresses to wear while we prayed over the patient. When we finished, from her sick bed the mother looked up and remarked, 'Sister, that dress of mine fits you perfectly. Why don't you keep it, and just say a tiny prayer for me every time you put it on?" It didn't take me long to see the Lord's hand in this surprise. "Good Lord, you've had your way again" Here was the light-weight clothing for which I had prayed the previous night. My God had not only granted my request but besides He dressed me up in real style !

DAY ONE : TRUSTING

One Pair Of Blue Pants And A Bible, Lord !

(4) Speaking of the poor and their trust in God, one of the most delightful answers to prayer I've seen is what happened to a five year old student of mine, Samir by name. He was a Christian of Scheduled Caste background. At the time of this incident he was in my Montessori III class. One day a schoolmate of Samir, who was from a rich family, wore to school a pair of foreign-made blue stretch pants. Samir fell in love with these pants and when classes were over he came to me and confided that he wanted a pair of pants just like those blue ones he had seen. Samir's mother was a domestic servant in our school and I knew she didn't have the means to buy clothes of this sort, even if they were available on our Indian market which they weren't. My response to Samir's petition was that he should speak to his Heavenly Father. This tiny kid took me at my word and let me know a couple of times during the next few days that he was praying to the Father for those beautiful blue pants. The following week a Sister in our community received a package from Germany. I helped her open the package. It contained childrens' clothes and, lo and behold, among them was also a pair of practically brand new blue stretch pants. When I saw that they were exactly Samir's size, I knew this was an answer to a five year old's prayers. The pants were a heavenly gift, his dream come true. I gave the pants to his mother, who told me that as soon as she gave Samir this gift, he shouted, "See ! Heavenly Father has given me my blue pants !" He announced this to everyone he met. Next, he told his mother that he wanted a bible. She dismissed this as a child's whim and did not pay any attention. But Samir persisted and he added many tears to his request. A neighbour heard his crying and came over to ask what the fuss was about. When she heard what Samir was asking, she gve him her own copy of the bible in Hindi. Now the fun really began. Samir could not read SO, as soon as he received the Book, he asked his mother to read that story, which he had heard in school, about a lost sheep. She opened the bible at random and pretended to read the parable of the lost sheep. Because she was illiterate, she made up her own *naanee-kee-kahaanee* (grandmother's tale). Well, she had not

gone very far before Samir told her that she was not reading the right story. That night Samir insisted on sleeping with the bible under his pillow. Bright and very early next morning with the big Book under his arm Samir marched into the convent chapel while our sisters were still busy with their prayers. Samir asked a nun sitting near the chapel door to read him the story about the lost sheep. Recognising Samir as one of my Montessori students, she called me. I quietly ushered him out of the chapel and asked him what the matter was that brought him to school so early. When he expressed his desire to hear about "that lost sheep", I found the place in Luke 15 and read the story to him. He listened with full attention. I thought this would end the episode; but it did not. He began to tell his family members and classmates that the Heavenly Father would give them anything they asked. Samir turned into a convinced messenger of God's goodnews.

When I reflect on Samir's faith, and how he received his blue pants and bible, there comes to mind a picture of Jesus with little children. He holds up one lovingly to me and other adults as a model of undoubting trustfulness. I believe the Lord wants all people of all ages and religions to possess Samir's kind of trust in God our Father's tender, abundant love for each of us. But only those who ask Him will see and recognise these mini- miracles as they occur in our daily lives. So I say, *"Blessed are those who know they are poor and know they need God !"* The poor in spirit know how to call on God. By the "poor" I mean those who are lovingly dependent upon the Lord for everything, spiritual and material. This is the reason, I think, why as a class of people the financially poor welcome Christ's joy full message. Rich people do not feel the constant need of God. They do not have to pray for their "daily bread". Their drinking water, clothing, housing and medical care are mostly taken for granted. It is the poor, however, who must daily ask for these necessities. As I read the bible, especially the gospels, I see Jesus as a brother-to-all, a man who lives among the poor, as one of them. He understands them and they Him. This is the way it has been for almost two thousand years. His loving power makes the poor rich in trusting faith.

DAY ONE : TRUSTING

Those Who Trust Only In Making Money

(5) I usually conclude my illustrations by relating how I was made a dupe of someone's greedy trickery. I do this because there are plenty of folks who see themselves as having been victimised; and they use these painful episodes as reasons not to trust others. They become cynical and hypercritical of everyone in need. This is a mistaken and very sad reaction.

Anyone who has travelled to Madras by train in the early 1980's has probably heard of Moore Market, which used to be just next to the railway station. Before this place was burnt down to be replaced by a large government building, it was famous for offering almost anything a traveller would want to buy at cheap prices. Passing through Madras once, I found that between train connections I had over an hour to spare; so my companion and I decided to visit Moore Market's many shops just to see what was available. I ended up purchasing a towel for five rupees and my friend bought some talcum powder for Rs. twenty. After a couple of hours on our train journey I decided to wash up a bit, using my new towel. To my disappointment I discovered that when the towel came into contact with water its bright green colour drained away and turned into a sickly yellow. Examining the texture closely I noticed that all of the threads were loose and easily came apart. After only a single use ! I told my friend about my mistake; so she took out her new talc powder to find that there was a thin top layer of real talcum and underneath was wheat dust. As the two of us lamented and expressed our disillusionment, I heard other passengers cursing the Moore Market shop owners for having cheated them, too. Those Madras merchants were earning a daily living through trickery. Their cleverness included a smiling face and words of service. But in their hearts they had placed as their first priority a principle of profit-by-any-means. Day after day they earned their wealth by fraud-even though it meant forever losing their customers' trust. Nursing my hurt pride and anger that night on the train as we headed towards Calcutta, I imagined the Moore Marketeers enjoying their evening meals while having a big laugh over how they had fooled so many people. At a deeper level, however, I could not help

A TIME FOR HEALING

aksing who really are the fools? Who will have the last laugh? Are these not "cleaver" money-makers actually destroying themselves and their families by a vicious value system of worshipping money? I determined not to let this Moore Market experience turn my journey sour or make me suspicious of every seller.

Sharings of this sort by one or other retreat facilitator serves a double purpose both as witness and animation of retreatants on how to trust the group with our own vulnerability. This session concludes with each participant telling the person next to them something about her/his own early experiences of trust within their immediate family circle of parents, brothers and sisters. After each partner shares, we encourage them to pary together for relatives, living and departed. Through the communion-of- saints these relatives are actively interested in and interceding for this retreat, which includes healing of family relationships.

* Holy Hour: A full sixty minutes is dedicated to adoration before the Blessed Sacrament exposed. It is spent mostly in silence, with as little structure as possible. One of the animators reads John 1:35-51, which describes Christ's call of his first disciples. After reading this passage the animator invites the group to pray silently for each other by asking the Lord through His Spirit to help everyone present to become a more trusting companion. The list of sharing teams is known by this time; each partner is encouraged to keep her/his companion before the Lord. Like the first disciples we want to discover the Messiah within this trusting community.

* Common Reflection III : This session focuses on PEACE (see Jn 14:27). It is a most precious gift for which our world today, everyone everywhere, yearns and searches. When you ask people what they most want, this gift is the constant response: PEACE ! Our human family experiences much suffering, injustice, and anxiety, perhaps more today than ever before. As a global village, we begin very slowly to learn that each of us must contribute something in order to achieve world peace. It is more and more clear that peace has a "price tag" on it. It costs something. It makes demands upon us for deep changes within us and within our own communities. But we are not always so clear where to begin changing and seeking this basic union and harmony without which life is not worth living. About fifty years ago, certain psychiatrists talked as though they had the big answer, the key to this quest for peace. Half-a- century later we are certain that psycho-analysis will *not* heal our broken, tense world. As the late psychiatrist and priest Ignace Lepp observes, the proper role of psychiatry is to show us where we are wounded, so that we may bring these wounds to the Lord to heal. The very expensive nature of Freudian psychology in terms of money and time has made it obvious that there has to be a more available instrument of emotional and mental health for the masses of people.

Transactional Analysis And Deeper Healing

Transactional Analysis came on the scene as a more available and much less expensive therapy. T.A., as it came to be known, popularised the basic insights of psychiatry so that they were within the comprehension of ordinary people of moderate education. T.A. workshops, seminars and literature brought to millions of mentally and emotionally disturbed persons an easy-to-understand, a do-it-together therapy. T.A. has helped people become aware of the concepts of root-feelings and root-memories. In this way it has offered them optional ways of looking at and responding to reality, of being more responsible for the way they think, feel and act in their relationships with others, themselves and God.

The fad-phase of T.A. was symbolised by paperback bestsellers like "I'm O.K., You're O.K." and "What Do You Say After You Say Hello?". You will not find these volumes on bookshop shelves today. They are gone. But there are plenty of other books to take their place. Some are no more than quick-fix formulas to health and happiness. Such books appeal to those in search of superficial, painless short-cuts to healing our human ills. There are, however, other solid, successful guidelines for those thoughtful persons who are willing to work at their own growth. As for T.A., it remains a reliable help for understanding and effectively dealing with many of our interpersonal tensions--provided we recognise its limitations and are ready to work hard, cooperating with others and with God's grace. Applying T.A. with expert help we can begin to move out of the guagmire of mixed emotions that has kept so many of us prisoners for so long. After fifteen years of using T.A., I have come to realise that authentic healing can come about through a combination of T.A. and inner healing. The Lord Jesus alone heals. But He wants us to use all proper resources which are available to us. Inner healing means using skills and insights of behavioural sciences but also going beyond them by recourse to individual and community prayer, by "soaking" the patient in God's love. Inner healing also includes guidance from the inspired Word of Scripture, as we shall see in this retreat.

T.A. In God's Service

I see clearly that the Lord is utilising applied psychology today as an instrument of healing. In inner healing retreats we employ T.A. concepts to help people towards greater understanding of mind and heart and, therefore, towards greater personal growth. In IHRs I have observed so many people come to a strong awareness that change for wholeness is available through learning that there are more ways than one to respond to dysfunctional relationships and painful, unjust social situations. In IHRs there is generated a strong consciousness and conviction that we can grow inwardly mentally, emotionally, spiritually. This awareness comes about within a faith-community that prays and worships together. As one family the retreat group moves ahead, dependent upon each other's support and the power from the Lord's Spirit. Personnal growth and inner freedom are fostered in IHRs through skilled counselling and the personal concern of others, people pursuing peace by mutual trust.

Early Nurturing And Its Consequences

We may have heard the half-comic, half-cynic remark, "I love humanity; it's people that I can't stand !" Most of us have trouble not with things in general but with persons in particular. What do we "do" with people--starting with ourselves? Here's where the

DAY ONE : TRUSTING

struggle with reality comes. Do we dare look honestly at ourselves and our family of origin? We of the twentieth century have the Human Sciences to thank for helping us to see the importance in our lives of feelings, emotions, and early relationships. T.A. offers us ways to trace back many of these feelings, especially the negative ones, to their sources. Not a few of the unquestioned beliefs upon which we model much of our behaviour come not from divine revelation but from distorted and often contradictory perceptions of our parents and elders. T.A. also helps us explore our unhealthy patterns of thoughts-feelings-behaviour, which it calls "games". Analysing them we can see ourselves more objectively. We can also see the crooked little tricks we unconsciously played upon ourselves and others in order to survive. These "games" are ways of coping with difficult situations. They are not the truth-in-love but double-dealing modes of behaviour we learned in early childhood and which we are still unconsciously using as adults. And this, despite the fact that these ways of relating are unhelpful and self-defeating. More seriously, these ulterior motive behaviours can and do influence life in ways that are harmful and destructive. T.A. uncovers unhealthy "life position" and "life-scripts"; it offers us more realistic and more loving inner attitudes that favour peace within ourselves and our communities.

Four Basic Life-Positions

There are four basic life-positions which are expressed by T.A. in this way

    (1)   I'm not O.K; You're O.K

    (2)   I'm not O.K.; You're not O.K.

    (3)   I'm O.K.; You're not O.K.

    (4)   I'm O.K.; You're O.K.

The word "O.K." as used in T.A. is difficult to translate by one word. It stands for a sense of being adequate, loved, valued and unconditionally accepted. This mental-emotional position is arrived at by a decision made consciously or unconsciously. In early life the basic life-position is largely influenced by the way the person has received

A TIME FOR HEALING

"strokes" and/or has evaluated those strokes--from others, especially from the very important persons in their lives (parents, relatives and close neighbours). It follows immediately that the way this person has been stroked (positively, negatively, physically/emotionally), in that very way will the person tend to stroke--inter--relate with--others. Stated briefly, the O.K. child comes from a warm, positive family environment; the not-O.K. child is product of negative nurturing.

> *If a child lives with criticism, it learns to condemn.*
> *If a child lives with hostility, it learns to fight.*
> *If a child lives with fear, it learns to be apprehensive.*
> *If a child lives with pitying, it learns to feel sorry for itself.*
> *If a child lives with ridicule, it learns to be shy.*
> *If a child lives with jealousy, it learns to envy.*
> *If a child lives with shame, it learns to feel guilty.*

The predominant feelings of this kind of child grown into an adult will be negative. As T.A. puts it, such a person will have a lot of "brown stamps", which she/he has collected from perceived destructive ways of inter-relating. Such a person's basic orientation will be life-denying. The O.K. person, on the other hand, blossoms out from positive, loving relationships. The O.K. person is life-affirming, because:

> *If a child lives with encouragement, it learns to be confident.*
> *If a child lives with tolerance, it learns to be tolerant.*
> *If a child lives with praise, it learns to be appreciative.*
> *If a child lives with acceptance, it learns to love.*
> *If a child lives with approval, it learns to like itself.*
> *If a child lives with recognition, it learns it's good to have a goal.*
> *If a child lves with sharing, it learns about generosity.*
> *If a child lives with honesty and fairness, it learns what truth and justice are.*

DAY ONE :   TRUSTING

If a child lives with security, it learns to have faith in itself and those around it.

If a child lives with friendliness, it learns that the world is a nice place in which to live.

If you live with serenity, the children around you will live in peace of mind and heart.

Feelings That Are Golden Stamps

The feelings that go with a life-position of "I'am O.K.; You're O.K." are called "golden stamps". These are collected within a family atmosphere that is warm, nurturing and loving. I am well aware that very few of us have been brought up in an ideal family. As we enter adulthood! most people from their early childhood have a mixed collection of feelings, some that are "golden stamps" and some-- maybe many--"brown stamps" too. In the search for peace and salvation, we need learn to surrender our pasts to the Lord, thanking Him for being our Saviour and aksing Him to heal that past. We have a right as God's beloved children to enjoy that freedom which has been purchased so dearly by Christ. It is only in this inner freedom that we can serve Him and others with love. So, in an IHR we spend much time reflecting upon early experiences, becoming aware of the nurturing or lack of it which we received as children. Our scope is not limited to "looking for trouble", nor is it restricted to family relationships. During these days of retreat we want to review with gratitude the tremendous love God has showered on us through Jesus and the Spirit, through the sacraments, through parents, relatives and friends. The Good News with which we have been gifted through baptism and the church community's own concern for us is the most powerful reason for us to be confirmed in our identity--and our decision--of being God's family. Despite our failings, limitations and sins, we are called to experience a deep sense of being O.K. This comes from our own decision towards ourselves and towards others, who are also redeemed by Christ. What we say of ourselves, we proclaim joyfully of every human being:

A TIME FOR HEALING

I may be young, I may be old, but I'm somebody--for, I'm God's child!

I may be educated, I may be uneducated, but I'm somebody--for, I'm God's child!

I may be brown or black or white, but I'm somebody--for, I'm God's child!

I may be poor, I may be rich, but I'm somebody--for I'm God's child!

I may be thin, I may be fat, but I'm somebody--for, I'm God's child!

I may be married, I may be divorced, but I'm somebody--for, I'am God's child!

I may be single, I may be widowed, but I'm somebody--for, I'm God's child!

I may be successful, I may be a failure, but I'm somebody--for, I'm God's child!

I may be a sinner, I may be a saint, but I'm somebody--for, I'm God's child!

For, Jesus is my Saviour and I'm God's child!

It is not easy to turn off destructive self-talk within us, if we are not aware of a number of facts.

(1) First of all, the habit of negative reflections are a *learned behaviour* they are not born with us, nor are they necessary.

(2) Another thing we have to become aware of is that consciously or unconsciously *we ourselves have made decisions* to listen to these inner messages, to have these attitudes and to follow these behaviours which are life-denying.

(3) The not-O.K. positions for ourselves and others have been, by and large, arrived at through painful experiences in childhood. These positions have been arrived at through *negative stroking received from adults around us.*

DAY ONE : TRUSTING

(4) T.A. tells us that to a surprisingly large degree our affective lives, perceptions and inter personal relationships with others family and world have been shaped according to a pattern, a "life script", *which we unconsciously chose for ourselves* very early in our lives, probably before the age of five.

(5) Our minds, like wondrous video-cassette recorders, have stored up these happenings, *as we have perceived them distortions and all.* After these formative years our life-experiences have been selectively interpreted according to early decisions: I'm O.K., I'm not O.K., You're O.K. You're not O.K.

Believing The Bad News Or Good News ?

The work of this retreat we can explain as one of being evangelised anew, of deciding afresh what we are going to believe: either the bad-news of our wounded memories or the good-news of God's Holy Spirit within us. Christ, the Prince of Peace, comes inviting us to let the truth set us free. To pronounce our own free "yes" to reality means saying "no" to untruth, to archaic, distorting messages that we have come to take for granted. Each member of our wounded human family is like Rapunzel, the fairy tale maiden, who had come under the influence of an evil witch. This "auntie" witch had imprisoned her by telling vicious lie The witch kept telling Rapunzel that she was the most ugly person in the whole world--when, in fact, she was a very beautiful maiden. This evil "auntie" built up around the young girl an atmosphere of terror, saying that Rapunzel's very appearance would cause others to die of fright. So, Rapunzel was made to believe that she must hide herself from others. She obeyed this false injunction for a long time, until one day a wounderful Prince came into the jungle on a hunting trip. The two young people met face-to-face and it was love at first sight. When Rapunzel realised what was happening, she ran away in fright, lest her looks kill the young man by her ugliness. This tale is a parable for today. It is not didfficult to identify Christ as the Prince who ultimately frees the victim Rapunzel by revealing the turth about herself and his love of her. Rapunzel's inner struggle is the basic conflict within every person's heart. Is she to believe the witch's ugly

A TIME FOR HEALING

story or is she to turst the Prince's word, which alone will set her free ? Our crucified–risen Lord has paid a tremendous price to come to us today to bring us the messsage of pecae and salvation:

> *The time is fulfilled, and the kingdom of God is close at hand. Repent and believe the gospel.* (Mk. 1:15)

Repentance means deliberately *turning from*: our old, false ways, distorted thoughts, negative feelings, manipulative behaviour. Repentance implies resolutely *turning to:* the sunshine of life and peace. Finally, repentance entails *surrendering and committing ourselves* unconditionally to the Lord and His truth. What M.Scott Peck describes as mental health applies to repentance as well. It is an "on-going process of dedication to reality at all costs."

During our retreat reflections we shall be using a number of helpful insights and exercises from T.A. These are tools that we use in our quest for that turth and life which our Lord promises us. We want to use everything which will help us know Him more clearly, love Him more dearly, and follow Him more nearly.

This third common reflection of Day one closes with a sharing by partners on anyone of the following topics:

(1) Describe the journey which brought you to this retreat. What do you best remember about it and why?

(2) What is your present work/occupation? How did you get involved in it? Describe how it promotes happiness and peace in yourself and others.

(3) Share a recent misunderstanding that you had with another person. What sort of "strokes" were used (negative or positive)? Has this misunderstanding been resolved? Why?

The retreatants end their sharing session by thanking the Lord together. Pray for each other and others in the group and remember the church and our country. (see psalm 122: *"I will pray for your well-being. I will say, 'Peace upon you!".*

DAY ONE : TRUSTING

* **Eucharistic Celebration :** As stated in the Introduction, the readings and Mass of the day are preferred. If an option is given, then a thematised celebration can be helpful, by selecting some key biblical texts which have been used during the common reflections. A suggested theme: praying in the power of Christ's Holy Spirit. A votive Mass of the Holy Spirit is recommended, using the first eucharistic prayer. Keeping in mind the aim of this day, the readings suggested are: (1) Rm 8:26-27; (2) Ps 42- 43; (3) Lk 11:9-13.

* **Night Common Sharing :** This session should last about an hour. It is facilitated by one of the staff memebrs. Its purpose is like that of a good charismatic prayer meeting, consisting of: (a) praising and thanking God our Father for His goodness to us and the world; (b) building up each other's faith by sharing our own; (c) using the Spirit's gifts and the experiences given us, because these are not just for ourselves but for service to the community. It is an unprogrammed procedure. Keeping the focus on what has happened in the retreat thus far, anyone may share their prayer, their views, their perceptions of this first day. Whoever facilitates, strives for two things: (1) to keep each person's contribution within the context of here-and-now; (2) to restrict each one to a presentation that is brief, so that as many people may share as possible. In other words, both individual and group needs have to be considered. So, the leader is careful to allow as much participation as possible, while maintaining a balance of praise and thanks, personal witness, and song. The session concludes with the animator offering a prayer in the name of all. The final announcement is to encourage retreatants to pay attention to their sleeping dreams. When they arise next morning, they can briefly jot down what the dream was about. Their efforts to "catch a dream" will be reported and discussed the follwing day.

* **Team Evaluation :** As for all retreats so too an IHR strives to be open to the Spirit's guidance by careful discernment. This calls for free sharing among staff memebers on what is happening within the community. Of course, strict confidentiality is observed for anything learned in one-to-one guidance sessions. The best time

A TIME FOR HEALING

for this team meeting is at the day's end. It begins and ends with spontaneous thanksgiving prayer by the whole team. The next day's theme for the eucharistic celebration is decided. The animator for each common session is also designated.

PRAYER FOR THE GRACE TO TURST
(For Day One)

Abba, Father, I dare call You so/
Your goodness alone allows me now into your loving presence/
To be myself: without pretence, shame or fear of rejection/
Thank you for the joy of knowing You welcome me today as I am/
Jesus, pierced of heart on calvary cross to fill my heart/
For long days and nights I have yearned to trust/
Empower me to be honest with myself and You, without pretence/
In the cave of my heart so many times You've whispered/
"Don't fear!" And yet I do/
"Wy worry about food or clothing or anything?"
And yet I do/

Spirit of encouragement/
You're the One to fill all God's children with holy confidence/
Flow in me, wash my violating wounds too deep to tell/
I turst, but heal my lack of trust/Amen !

DAY TWO

A TIME FOR HEALING: BY LISTENING

> **The whole group of believers was united, heart and soul.... None of their members was ever in want.... Each day, with one heart, they regularly went to the Temple but met in their houses for the breaking of bread; they shared their food gladly and generously; they praised God and were looked up to by everyone.** (Ac. 4:32,34; 2:46)

* **Aim of the Day :** (a) To discover some of the rewards of listening with the heart to others--including oneself and God; (b) to move towards becoming a community in which persons are more concerned with serving their neighbours' needs rather than being just anxious over the fulfillment of their own wants.

* **Morning Prayer :** Psalm 95 *("Come, let us cry out with joy to Yahweh....").* Originally a processional hymn, it is a passionate invitation to God's priestly, prophetic people to listen-in-faith and to praise with all their hearts. Around the world each day, until the Lord Jesus' Second Coming, the pilgrim church fittingly begins her prayer with this psalm. As we begin Day Two we pay special attention to verses 7-8.

> *If only you would listen to him today !*
> *Do not harden your hearts.....*

Perhaps we too easily exempt ourselves from being in this class of hardened hearts. All of us like to consider ourselves as being good-listeners. But, in fact, are we? With everyone? We've heard it said that familiarity breeds contempt. An attitude of only half listening--or even quarter-listening--is indeed an expression of proud disdain. Am I selective in my listening, picking and choosing those to whom I listen attentively with my whole heart? Today we want the grace to be sincere with ourselves, brave enough to examine our quality of listening. This starts with our daily listening to those immediately around us. And, to be sure, this includes our faith- listening. This means listening-in-depth, listening beneath the superficial to the level at which we meet the real person. Like trusting, listening is a central biblical theme.

A Father And Son Who Listen To Each Other

In all gospel accounts God the Father is portrayed as being constantly and lovingly attentive to Jesus' needs: *"Father, I thank you for hearing my prayer. I myself knew that you hear me always..."* (Jn 11:41-42). Servant and Son, Jesus is shown as habitually looking and listening unto His *Abba,* eager to obey His plan in every detail of His Life. Already at the age of twelve Jesus is described as alert to His Father's inspiration, and so He stayed in the temple--even though it also meant temporarily hurting the feelings of Mary and Joseph. Having ritually celebrated His coming-of-age in the Bar Mitzvah ceremony, Jesus spends His time now listening to the teachers and respectfully asking them questions. (Lk 2:41-50).

The Paraclete Who Listens Completely

We notice how Jesus reveals the "Other Paraclete" as one who first of all listens perfectly to the Father and Son:

> *When the Spirit of truth comes he will lead you to the complete turth, since He will lead you to the complete truth, since he will not be speaking of his own accord, but will say only what he has been told; and he will reveal to you the things to come. He will glorify me, since all he reveals to you will be taken from what is mine.*
> (Jn 16:13-15)

DAY TWO : LISTENING

These revelations of God as a Trinity of listening Persons have very practical implications for us who are striving to build a healing community not only in this retreat but in our lives as well. Our human origin and goal are within this divine community of total giving and receiving. So, from all eternity we are destined ultimately for *perfect listening.* Our final fulfilment will consist in this *total listening and responding with all our hearts.*

Model For Disciples, Mary, The Listener

The very first Christian is Mary of Nazareth. Especially by gospeller artist, St. Luke, Mary is pictured as treasuring and constantly pondering the mystery of Christ in her heart. She listened to Jesus' words and events; she believed and trusted-- even though she did not always understand. As for all of us, life for Mary was an uneven journey, one day at a time, and often one step at a time.

All true disciples are characterised as obedient listeners. This is the meaning of "saving-faith": hearing God's Word as His message and putting it into practice in our lives with complete surrender of ourselves (see Rm 1:5;10:14f). In the renewed rite of christian initiation, the baptising priest symbolically touches the right and left ears of the newly baptised. At the same time he pronounces the word which Jesus used over the deaf man, *"Ephphatha', that is, 'Be opened'"* (Mk 7:35), so that the disciple may now listen to the Good News, believe it and follow it faithfully. Since the coming of Jesus Christ we live in *Anno Domini,* the year of our Lord. This is the messianic era promised by Old Testament prophets. By the gift of faith people are able to hear God's Word with "ears of the heart" so as to hear, recognise and respond to marvellous, inaudible and invisible realities--the mysteries of God's Kingdom. In Vatican II's *Constitution on Divine Revelation* Christ's community of disciples is described as primarily hearing the Word of God with reverence and proclaiming it with faith (see para 1). In the *Constitution Of The Church In The Modern World* the Church is also shown as listening to God speaking to us in our era's events, needs and longings (see para 11). The Council tells us that God addresses us today in every reality within us and around us. It is by listening-in-faith that the

Church can discern in all these happenings the signs of God's presence and purpose.

The Tragedy Of Not Listening

In all human dealings non-listening by one or both parties means a breakdown in communication and death to the relationship. Refusing to listen to another person signifies hostility and defiance. No surprise that the prophets refer to rebellion against God in terms of refusal to listen:

> Look, their ears are uncircumcised, they cannot listen. Look, for them Yahweh's word is something to sneer at, they have no taste for it. (Jr. 6:10)

Only God can open hearts, minds and ears for us to hear and to understand:

> Morning by Morning Yahweh makes my ear alert to listen like a disciple. Lord Yehweh has opened my ear and I have not resisted, I have not turned away. (Is 50:4-5)

> Jesus then opened their minds to understand the scriptures. (Lk 24:45)

> Lydia listened to us, and the Lord opened her heart to accept what Paul was saying. (Ac 16:14)

It has been said that the rock-bottom struggle of every human being is with the fear of not being accepted, fear of not being able to cope with life and fear of not being loved. As we begin this second day of our retreat we hear the Lord reminding us that *He wants to be accepted by us*, by our listening hearts:

> If only you would listen to me today! Do not harden your hearts as you have done so many times before--out of fear or resentment or disdain. Let go of this old habit of non-listening. Let me be your Saviour ! Listen and believe so that you may learn that I am your God!

DAY TWO : LISTENING

*Meditation : After breakfast for one hour each day of our IHR retreatants are encouraged to spend time alone with the Lord. The animator begins with a few moments of relaxing and loosening up exercises through deep breathing. This is combined with use of a Christian *mantraa* or ejaculation.. Today's meditation begins with the *Jesus Prayer* (Mk 10:48). The sacred syllables are uttered inaudibly. Inhaling, *"Je......"* and exhaling, *"... sus!"* After some moments of doing this, the full prayer is repeated. Inhaling and interiorly thinking of the sacred name, *"Jesus, Son of David..."* and exhaling, *"...have pity on me!"* (or an alternative, *"Jesus, son of Mary, mercy me a sinner !)* About five minutes is devoted to this centering prayer, then St. Luke's parable of the tax collector and pharisee is read (see Lk 18:9-14). After this the group is left by itself to complete the hour in silent meditation.

* Common Reflection I: The session begins with volunteers sharing what they recall of their previous night's dream/s. Staff members help the group discover what these dreams mean. Dreams contain much rich symbolism. This supports a number of facts: (1) every person naturally is a symbol-maker; (2) important communication is done not so much in literal but in symbolic language. With a little study and experience, everyone can learn what dream symbols mean so as to decipher their messages. When we "catch a dream" by recalling and analysing it, we will discover how dreams bring into our awareness areas of ourselves that we had not noticed. After we analyse our dreams we can then offer to the Lord what needs to be healed or strengthened for service to others. Each morning of the retreat we spend 10-15 minutes on this new skill of "catching dreams".

Next we focus upon the day's theme: our community called to listen-in-depth. As a help to get started reflecting on this topic, we sometimes use the "Johari Window" exercise. Its purpose is to help people become aware that communication within a group depends upon two factors: (1) individuals ready and willing to open the "windows" of their personalities and lives in order to let others know who they are, and (2) the group ready and willing to give feedback to the individual on what it knows of the individual and how it responds to her/him. The Johari Window is a useful instrument for understanding that our communities grow in personal relationships on the basis of how well we reveal our thoughts/ feelings and how much feedback we give/receive in an authentic listening community.

Jesus' Listening And Giving Feedback

A striking example of this "give-and-take" of community is found when Jesus questions his disciples, *"Who do you say I am?"* They had heard many wild, bazaar rumours about their Master, *"Some say (that you, Jesus are) John the Baptist, some Elijah, and others Jermiah or one of the prophets."* But Peter was not fooled by these false notions of the crowds. He listened-in- faith in order to learn Jesus' true identity, *"You are the Christ, the Son of the living God"* (Mt 16:16). Jesus at once confirms this description of who He really is, *"Simon, son of Jonah, you're a blessed man ! Because it was no human agency that revealed this to you but my Father in heaven."* Here is an interaction of truth in love. By his very pointed query Christ first evokes Peter's feedback and then confirms it as accurate. This in turn leads to another self revelation by Jesus, while at the same time He gives feedback to Peter as to his God-given indentity and mission, *"So i now say to you: You are Peter and on this rock I will build my community. And the gates of the underworld can never overpower it. I will give you the keys of the kingdom of Heaven: whatever you bind on earth will be bound in heaven; whatever you loose on earth will be loosed in heaven"* (Mt 16:18-20). This is a model for personal sharing. Affirming-listening and confirming-feedback lead to deeper bonds of faith and friendship. For sure, the Johari Window was not designed to tell us why people do not share themselves. Nor does it explain why others do not "listen straight" to their neighbours' messages of self-revelation. This is where Transactional Analysis (T.A.) comes to our aid.

T.A. And The Quality Of Our Listening

The quality of listening between two persons or within a community is the measure of interpersonal relationships. Transactional

DAY TWO : LISTENING

Analysis helps us analyse what goes right and wrong in our listening patterns. If there is love between persons, there will be good listening. If there is fear, hate or indifference, listening will be distorted and defective. The topic and circumstances in which the communication takes place also influence the kind of listening. It tends to get jumbled if the subject is highly emotional, or discussed with plenty of negative feelings, as is done, for example, in a quarrel. But it is not just the relationship, topic or circumstances which confuse human transactions. Listening is much more mysterious.

The Community Of Persons Within Each Of Us

Every person carries around within them a whole community of life--long personal relationships. Each relationship has its own history. No matter how many years ago these significant relationships were begun, they can and do affect the way we listen today. T.A. identifies three main "ego-states", which influence a person's listening and speaking. these "states" are consistent patterns of thoughts and feelings that relate to corresponding patterns of behaviour. One of the founders of T.A., Dr. Eric Berne, describes each state. (1) THE PARENT : Much of this ego-state's content is borrowed from parental figures. This state may function as a directing influence (called the "Influencing Parent"). It is also exhibited as imitating perceived parental behaviour (the "Active Parent"). It can be nurturing or controlling. In it are video recordings, as it were, of external events, that happened very early in a young person's life. These images and teachings are not questioned or criticised. They are the "parent tapes" sequences of the child's perceptions of its parents, as nurturing, disciplining, criticising, guiding and teaching them. This is why the Parent State is said to make up that concept of life which has been *taught*.
(2) THE ADULT : This state is oriented toward objective data-processing, like a computer which organises facts and tests them. It is that concept of life which is *thought*. (3) THE CHILD : As distinguished from the Adult Ego-State, the Child State is our concept of life which is *felt*. It is composed of memories, like video-tapes, of internal events early in llife, which are the child's responses to events around it, *the child's felt perceptions of reality.*

A TIME FOR HEALING

What is called the "Adapted Child" is modelled upon perceived parental teachings, the do's and don'ts. Another expression of this state is termed the "Natural Child". It is that part of the child's personality which is autonomous, spontaneous, free, creative and curious. These three states are all active within the first months of human life, certainly within the first year. They correspond to the Freudian division of personality division: *super-ego, and the id.* The Parent, Adult and Child analysis is illustrated by three identical circles one on top of the other, touching each other only at one point.

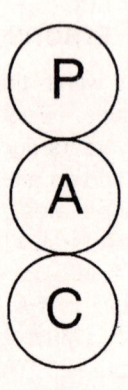

```
    P
    A
    C
```

We may well ask ourselves as we listen to different people in this retreat community, "Am I listening-straight, or am I imposing my own inner tapes upon what I am hearing?" In other words, "Is reality getting through to me, or am I actually listening to old messages from my Parent and Child ego-states?" If there is a "contamination" of information, this is diagrammed so that either the Parent or Child or circles are shown as invading the Adult circle.

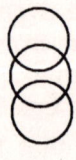

DAY TWO : LISTENING

With God Are We Listening Straight ?

Equally disturbing to us should be another question: "Am I hearing what God is saying to me in prayer or am I, instead, actually listening to my old tapes from my Parent-child experiences?"

To give the retreatants a sense of what it means to listen from different ego-states, we demonstrate with a small exercise. Five chairs are arranged in a row. Each is tagged with a different title : (1) NURTURING PARENT, (2) DISCIPLINING PARENT, (3) ADULT, (4) NATURAL CHILD, and (5) ADAPTED CHILD. Five volunteers sit on these chairs and repeat a simple phrase according to the ego- state tag which is on their chair. These volunteers are asked to demonstrate the ego state with a typical tone of voice, gesture, facial expression, thought and feeling. Any sentence may be used, for example:

"You see, I am sitting quietly with the Lord"

(1) The NURTURING PARENT position will speak the words encouragingly, comfortingly, communicating concern, warmth and love (2) the DISCIPLINING PARENT pronounces the same sentence sternly like pedagogue by implication, calling for compliance and immediate imitation. (3) The ADULT speaks the words in a manner that is objective, matter-of-fact, emotionally neutral. (4) The NATURAL CHILD position repeats this sentence with enthusiasm, spontaneity, as a child who is happily doing his/her own thing. (5) The ADAPTED CHILD, however, pronounces the words compliantly, carefullly, so as to get it correctly, like every "good child", who is anxious to please its parents.

It is important to point out that each volunteer of the five ego- states hears the words and repeats them exactly, word-for-word. But such superficial, verbal correctness is not all there is to human listening- -a computer is also verbally accurate. The five sentences are identical. But, since they are spoken from five different ego-states, they give to these same set of words five very different meanings. This is made even more complex when we consider that one PAC speaks to another PAC. The speaker may intend, consciously or

A TIME FOR HEALING

unconsciously, to address the other person from a certain ego-state. Due to many reasons, however, the hearer may listen in an ego-state not intended by the speaker. This is the origin of many misunderstandings. The speaker's spoken message and the hearer's response is known in T.A. as a "transaction". It is the unit of social interaction. Technically, it means that a transactional stimulus (e.g. the statement, "You see, I am sitting quietly with the Lord!") is spoken from a certain ego-state, and the listener responds from any of the five ego-states. This is a completed transaction. According to T.A. transactions are of three different kinds.

Three Kinds Of Transactions

"Transactions" in T.A. are classified and diagrammed as "parallel", "crossed", and "ulterior". (1) PARALLEL transactions go as smoothly and harmoniously as parallel lines. E.g. adult-to-adult and vice versa, parent-to-child and vice versa, etc.

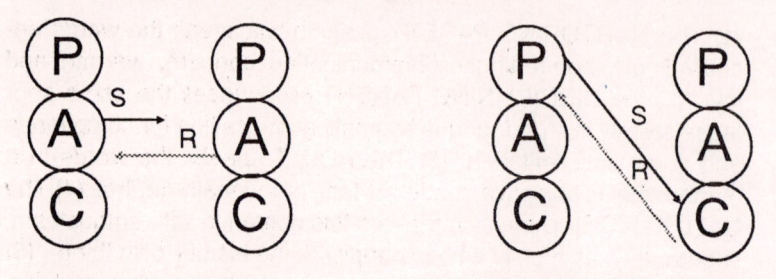

(2) CROSSED transactions, however, create sparks and conflict. E.g. parent-to-child as stimulus, and as response parent-to-child.

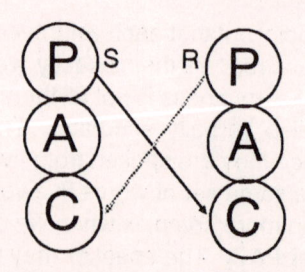

DAY TWO : LISTENING

(3) ULTERIOR transactions also include "GAMES". They are double level communications. One level is overt, social and conscious; the other level is covert, psychological--and maybe unconscious. E.g. stimulus one may be overtly adult-to-adult, but covertly there is another communication (stimulus two) which is parent-to-child. If the listener is "hooked" into the speaker's game, the response may be child-to-parent, which leaves the listener feeling tricked and put-down.

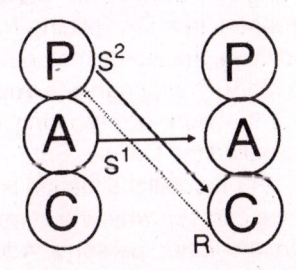

Different Ego-States For Different Transactions

Let's take our sample sentence, "You see, I am sitting quietly with the Lord." This is a statement of fact. When it is spoken from the Adult State, it is pronounced with a level tone, describing a piece of objective data. Sounds simple. But, the person listening to these words my be in any one of five ego- states. Because of this, the one hearing this declaratory sentence may get five different messages and complete the communication with anyone of the three kinds of transactions described above. So, the possible number of transactions are many. Let's see just a few of the possibilities.

(1) Listening and responding in a PARALLEL TRANSACTION : If the sentence is spoken in an adult ego-state and the listener responds from the same state, the transaction becomes PARALLEL, Adult-to-Adult. This response will have been with a simple nod of the head or by a simple assertion as, "I notice that." Diagrammed, the lines of stimulus and response move parallel to each other. There are many combinations of ego-states so as to have parallel transactions.

59

A TIME FOR HEALING

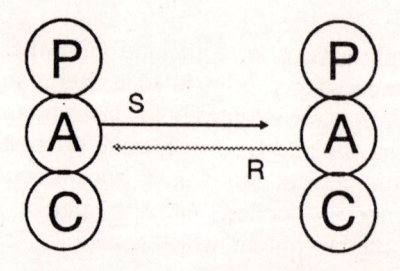

(2) Listening and responding in a CROSSED TRANSACTION : If the listener is, for some reason, in a Disciplining-Parent ego-state and responds from this position, the words may be more like those of a Martha admonishing Mary, "Yes, I can see you sitting quietly--while your sister does all the work of preparing the meal!" The Disciplining-Parent is also called the Critical- Parent. This transaction is called CROSSED; and a conflict situation is being built up. From the diagram below we can see why: the stimulus is from the Adult State addressed to the other person's Adult State. The response, however, crosses this up from another State, Parent-to-Child. Again, there are many combinations of ego-states of stimulus and response to produce a crossed transaction. Here we show only one example.

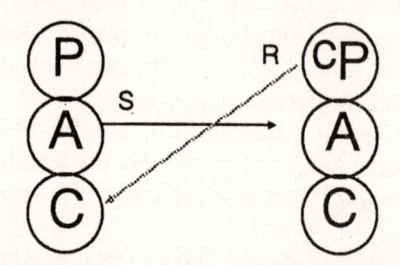

(3) Listening and responding in an ULTERIOR TRANSACTION : by the very name "ulterior" we are alerted to a double-message. One message (R-1) is from an overt ego-state; but the main message is sent from a covert ego-state (R-2) E.g. when Mary says to Martha, "You see, I am sitting quietly with the Lord," Martha responds, "And don't you see someone has to do all the work?" The overt message seems to be a question from the Adult State (R-1). Actually, the covert message is from the Disciplining or

60

DAY TWO : LISTENING

Critical-Parent ego-state (R-2). That this hidden message is the main transaction is very clear both from Martha's gesture pointing an accusing finger at Mary--and her scolding tone of voice. Martha is not really asking a question; she is telling Mary that she is a "lazy girl". This is why in the diagram R-2 is targeting Mary's Adopted Child ego-state. If Mary were to allow herself to get "hooked" into this game transaction of Martha, she would feel guilty. Being ashamed, she would then leave her Guest, go and help Martha. Martha, at the same time, is also feeling "bad" angry and indignant. In other words, in a "successful" ulterior transaction, all the "players" end up with bad feelings. Everyone loses!

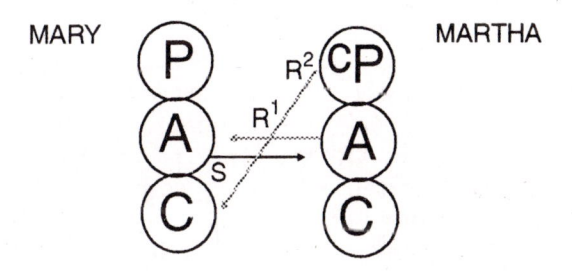

MARY   MARTHA

[Diagram: Two sets of stacked circles labeled P, A, C (Mary) and CP, A, C (Martha), with arrows labeled R^2, R^1, and S between them.]

Exercises For Building Awareness-In-Listening

The session concludes with partners sharing with each other. At the same time, this exercise helps them grow in awareness how each time they listen and responds to someone, they are in different ego-states. The following role-plays are suggestions :

* Allow yourself to go into your NURTURING PARENT; then jot down at least five good qualities which you recognise in yourself. Tell your partner about them, giving examples of how you use these gifts. Your partner is asked to listen in her/his Nurturing Parent, too. After five minutes or so, let the other partner share her/his good qualities.

* Going into your NATURAL CHILD consciousness, tell your partner some of your favourite childhood dreams and aspirations--the great things you aspired to do when you grew up. Give each partner an equal amount of time to share.

* Share some experiences of your ADAPTED CHILD--fears, anxieties, prohibitions given to you when you were very young and how you responded to them. Notice that while you are in this Child State, you not only recall ideas, but you relive the happening at your feeling level also. You again experience the power of our memories to recall the total event.

* **Common Reflection II** : The bible and behavioural science tell us in strong terms that each and every person on our planet is suffering. Not everyone may be aware of her/his pain, but it is a fact that we humans are in a state of constant suffering-- physical, mental, emotional, and spiritual. No one is exempt from this burden; we must carry it throughout our earthly pilgrimage. In an IHR we have the privilege first of listening to this suffering, not only within ourselves but also within our companions. A strong temptation is to avoid pain by keeping a safe distance from the suffering of others and of ourselves. Like that Jewish priest and levite in the Good Samaritan parable (see Lk 10:29-37), we may spend our lives passing by wounded travellers "on the other side". In this way we seek to avoid the responsibility of being involved with someone in critical need. As persons, however, we are called to be in a relation of openness to others. Vulnerability is the price to pay if we wish to live and grow. There is such a thing as *legitimate pain,* necessary pain, good pain. One important characteristic of mature persons is that they can and do overcome the fear of suffering in order to share the burden of other fellow travellers. This is what heroes and heroines are about. "No pain, no gain!" goes the old saying. Divine revelation informs us that the "other" is no stranger to us but part of ourselves:

> *Now Christ's body is yourselves, each of you with a part to play in the whole.* (1 Co 12:27)

There is another wise maxim, "To know all is to forgive all." When He was with us on this earth, Christ knew all and He forgave all. His sacred Heart was--and is--the most compassionate towards fellow human beings. He listens to the pain of His pilgrim sisters and brothers and helps carry their burdens.

DAY TWO : LISTENING

To Love Is To Listen Carefully

The retreat group has been together going on now two days. This is the proper time for us to greet everyone else, acknowledging them as members of one Body and accepting them unconditionally. I suggest a formula of greeting like this: "I accept and love you as part of myself in the Lord!" Perhaps some other words will be more culturally fitting. The point is that this ritual exchange is an *act of faith* in our communion within Christ which is itself rooted in our baptismal consecration, our anointing and indelible sealing by God's Holy Spirit.

> *It is God who gives us, with you, a sure place in Christ and has both anointed us and marked us with his seal, giving us as pledge the Spirit in our hearts.* (2 Co 1:21-22)

Implicit in this community-exchange is a promise of listening carefully to others. Put into other words, listening attentively is simply obedience to our Lord's command of loving others as He loves us (see Jn 15:12-17). Looking at each other and expressing christian love for each other seems strange and embarassing to some retreatants. The session animator does well to explicitate this block; examine it, take it seriously. For, every day at the eucharist the rite of peace is often omitted or else performed in an impersonal, meaningless manner. Perhaps not a few people associate expression of affection with trouble ! There is no doubt that mass media today romanticise and trivialise words like "love". As a result, this most beautiful four-letter word has been practically eliminated from some people's vocabulary, because it seems to them that "love" has mostly unwholesome meanings. The great doctor of the church, St. Thomas Aquinas, however, calls attention to the fact that "love" is not a feeling but an act of the will. It means: *to wish well to another and therefore to do good to that person.* Does it not seem absurd that although Jesus commands us to love one another, we do not express in words this christian affection even during the eucharist? The real test, of course, is that this ritual of peace and love in Christ be a FACT. Words are easy to say, deeds of witness are difficult. Both are needed: words that are followed by deeds. In this IHR we want to learn that Christ's commandment of love is fulfilled when we listen to others respectfully, even when it is difficult.

Our Prejudices As Blocks to Listening

When we are honest with ourselves and sensitive to the different movements within us, we come to recognise our own prejudices and jealousies. They are like scorching, destructive winds blowing across personal relationships. Unless we become conscious of these deadly forces, they will influence us as strong barriers to effective listening. Our most basic human fear is about whether we will be able to survive or not. This dread can grow and become a compulsion. It can goad us on to compete against others rather than to collaborate with them. Such a state of mind and heart can distort our vision of others so that neighbours look like enemies. Take the example of a drama. There are only a few main roles. All others are supporting parts, but all are necessary for successfully staging the story. This is reasonable. But our fear and pride demand at times either that WE play the lead role or else WE opt out! Our Rebellious Child ego-state demands the biggest and best, or else we refuse to co-operate. St. Paul uses a simile from the dining room: *"Not all the dishes in a large house are made of gold and silver; some are made of wood or earthenware...."* (2 Tm 2:20) As for plates fashioned by a careful artist, so for us designed by a loving Maker, Who shapes and ornaments us for different uses. These differences are not for privilege but service. And yet our pride is so easily hurt, when someone else is receiving attention and acclaim. Isn't the root of all this the fact that we compare superficial externals, while neglecting to see and appreciate our own inner beauty? *"Do not keep judging according to appearances; let your judgement be according to what is right."* (Jn 7:24)

Social sciences certainly confirm what God's Word tells us, that all of us are born into a wounded and broken situation. The Good News is that Christ has redeemed us. This does not mean that we do not have to work hard at living this re-creation, everyday claiming for ourselves His healing and liberating graces. Infant baptism, the other sacraments and family faith-nurturing do a tremendous amount to help us move from a not--OK position to perceiving ourselves and others as O.K.

From Basic Life-Position To Life-Script

We have already seen how very early in life we may unconsciously assume any one of three negative life-positions: (1) I'm not O.K., You're O.K.; (2) I'm O.K., You're not O.K.; (3) I'm not O.K., You're not O.K. Without awareness or conscious effort the young child in one or other of these basic positions designs a "life-script". This is very much like the scenario for a drama. It is a person's story plot based upon a life-position assumed in childhood and reinforced by the child's perceptions of family relationships. Let's hear a couple of biographical accounts to show how life-scripts are actually formed.

(1)   This is Susan's Story :

> During her pregnancy Susan's mother was yearning for and expecting a male child. Born a girl Susan was a big disappointment to her whole family. The general dissatisfaction over Susan's sex was communicated to her in many ways. Susan tried to cope with this impossible situation by making efforts to become O.K.--to earn her family's love and respect for not being a boy. Even as a small child Susan would contantly ask those around her after she completed any task, "Is it all right?" and "Do you like what I did?" Whenever someone of the family would express the slightest criticism or give a small sign of disapproval, Susan interpreted this as a rejection of herself as a person. Eventually Susan became chronically depressed and often physically sick.

COMMENT : Susan's life-script cast her in a tragic role of always working, day and night, never complaining, though others complained and criticised her. She was a "workaholic". She didn't serve freely or with love. She was driven by a compulsion to work harder and longer in order to arrive at that longed for but elusive state of pleasing everyone in order to feel O.K. What Susan did not realise was that very early in life, basing herself upon the way her family members seemed to reject her as a girl, she rejected herself as permanently not O.K. Her sternest critic, impossible to please, was herself. Without realising it, Susan was following a "counter-script". This is a life-plan based upon parental precepts. Susan's own personal life-script had her in the role of a loser, a not O.K. person. Her counter-script told her, *"Susan, you could be O.K., if only you would work very hard according to our liking !"* This scenario seems incredibly cruel and unreal. It is ! But, sad to say, there are many, many people who live their lives according to this kind of scripting. It is prepared in early childhood unconsciously but very consistently. It comes about from negative stroking by parents and near relatives. These are the people *who did not listen to a little girl who should-have-been a boy !* Those who do not know the real story-behind-the-story try to be helpful by telling the grown-up Susan, "Don't work so hard!" They tell her that she is crazy to slave away night and day. When a person like Susan, without any apparent reason, suddenly refuses to do any work at all, then everyone--including herself--is surprised. What actually happens is that Susan in desperation begins acting out an "anti-script". This is the exact opposite of everything she has perceived to be her life's directives from parents and family. Susan finally "revolts". She defies her perceived counter-script's impossible injunction to "work hard but never make it!" The Good News of Christ for Susan and all like her is this. Relationships that are based upon God's plan will set her radically free, allowing her to be her true self. The revelation of how she came to form her destructive life-script, counter- script, and anti-script will help liberate her from their destructive compulsions. Christ tells Susan and those suffering in similar circumstances--like India's more than ten crore Scheduled Castes, the ex-untouchables:

> *"If you make my word your home you will indeed be my disciples; you will come to know the truth, and the truth will set you free."* (Jn 8:31-32)
>
> *"I am the Way, I am Truth and Life."* (Jn 14:6)

(2) This is a young man's short life-history :

His name is Prem and he is a very bright, alert student in high school. He has been consistently a class leader, number one in most competitions. He has an authority problem with his parents and teachers--with anyone in a power position. He seems to enjoy publicly embarassing his elders showing them up as "stupid" at least in his estimation. Prem is popular with other youth, especially with those who are in tension with the establishment, like guardians, school and civic authorities. He likes to champion causes for the under-dog; he's ready to do anything so as to obtain justice. When school final examination results were published, there was a big surprise for Prem. He expected to get first division marks. He didnot. In fact, by a few marks he failed. This failure seemed to deflate him completely. He fell sick and withdrew from his friends entirely. He complained that he was unjustly disgraced. What particularly upset him was that while his companions were studying in college, he had to wait to write supplementary examinations.

With some bitterness he told his family that the reason for his failure was unjust marking by the examiners.

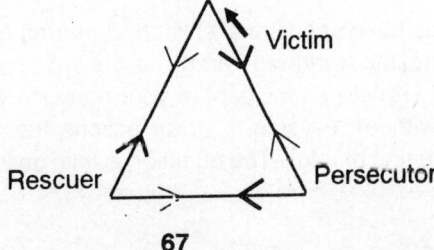

COMMENT : Prem's behviour and reactions can be understood if we look at the T.A. "Drama Triangle". This is an extremely useful concept created by Karpman. It is represented by an equilateral triangle whose corners are labelled "VICTIM", "PERSECUTOR" AND "RESCUER". These names describe roles both in game transactions and life-scripts. We have heard of a "vicious circle". This means a series of recurring events from which there is no escape, because the solution to one difficulty leads to another identical problem. Just so, this is a "vicious triangle" of not-O.K. ways of relating using the analogy of role-playing on the stage, Karpman's Drama Triangle demonstrates that a compulsive "Rescuer" can suddenly switch her/his role to play a "Persecutor" or "Victim". This is shown in the diagram by the reversed arrows, indicating that the player can move in either direction to take on the other two possible roles. Return to Prem's story. Before he failed his examination he seemed to be an O.K. personality, although he related to those in authority as being not O.K. In terms of the Drama Triangle, Prem regularly operated out of a "Rescuer" position. He compulsively and unconsciously was always on the lookout for someone who was being "persecuted", so that he could save this "Victim" from the "Persecutor". Analysing Prem's ego-state, he was O.K. but the victims and persecutors were not O.K. As he saw life, he was always "fixing up" others --defending his school friends and publicly ridiculing anyone in authority. But after Prem failed, he had to justify his life- position, "I'm O.K. (because I was *unjustly* failed); you're not O.K.' According to the Drama Triangle, Prem's habitual role was Rescuer--though towards authorities he was a Persecutor. When he failed in examinations, his role changed temporarily to that of Victim. From being an activist reformer, his social life turned in upon itself. He spent time wasting away, doing nothing, going nowhere, whimpering in self-pity and weak excuses.

This second reflection closes with group work as usual. sharing and listening is done on one or other of the following topics:

(1) The typical life-position emotionally of a child is "I'm not O.K., You're O.K." Not-O.K. children perceive themselves as Victims. Tell of a childhood experience in which you played the "Poor Me" game of someone who was victimised. While you were in this ego-state, tell how you related to your perceived Persecutor and Rescuer.

(2) All of us have seen small children nurturing each other, sometimes playing the Nurturing Parent, i.e. consoling other children who are crying. Relate an incident in your early life when you fulfilled this role, without realising it. Your actions then may have been appropriate and helpful. The question is this: do you know anyone-

DAY TWO : LISTENING

-including yourself--who plays the Rescuer's role? This means an adult who compulsively runs to the aid of other adults--unasked, unneeded, unhelpful? Do Rescuers of this kind really listen to other's words and actions, who try politely to inform the Rescuers that their help is not required? In answering, give an example from daily life.

(3) We all have some "Critical (Disciplining) Parent" within us. all we have to do is remember how our parents and elders taught us right from wrong, good from bad, etc. and then ask ourselves whether we imitate them when we offer correction to others. Share with your partner how you have played this role. In a game transaction, the Critical Parent is functioning as a Persecutor. As an adult, how do we listen/not listen while we are playing the Persecutor?

* HOLY HOUR : The animator recalls the aim of the day. It is to build an authentically listening community, which listens to others carefully. The prayer of listening is a prayer of attentive presence. We come before the Lord and simply listen and look unto Him. (See psalm 123: "I lift up my eyes to you who are enthroned in heaven....our eyes are on Yahweh our God, for Him to take pity on us.") Today's hour of adoration is an invitation to listen to the Lord with the ears-of-the-heart. By so doing, we allow God to fashion us into a community-in-the- Spirit, to be of one mind and one heart.

* COMMON REFLECTION III: A famous dramatist said that all the world is a stage and all people are players in a drama of life. We are discovering these days of retreat how true this is. god intends us to live our roles--our vocations--freely, with loving service. We are learning that often unaware we are playing roles that are not our real selves. Early in life as tiny tots we had to cope with difficult situations. In this coping we may have played "games" in order to survive and not to feel the pain of being not O.K. Chances are high that unless we have had a real conversion of mind and heart, we continue playing games today as adults. In T.A. language this means that we regularly use ulterior transaction that make everyone unhappy and feeling bad. The IHR helps us find out why we behave as we do and how we have options out of games. It is

A TIME FOR HEALING

consoling to know that even great saints also played games. Notice how clearly the different drama triangle roles appear in the following description of a famous gospel personality.

Peter Fisher's Story

Judging by his size, strength and vigorous behaviour, no one could doubt that Simon Peter Fisher considered himself very much of an O.K. person. At times, however, he was impulsive and overly blunt in speech. For example, one day when his Guru foretold that all His friends would run from Him in time of trouble, Peter protested, "Even if all fall away from You, I will never, I will never disown You." (Mt 26:35) Not long afterwards Peter and a group of his closest associates were taken by total surprise, when a police party along with a large, armed crowd came to arrest the Guru for questioning. Events moved swiftly. In an unsuccessful attempt to rescue his beloved Master, Peter used a deadly weapon and almost killed one of the crowd. Then in quick succession three times he publicly disowned having any knowledge of the Master. Finally, Peter ran away in fear, shame and tears.

COMMENT : As for a stage-drama or cinema, this gospel action has two sequences in two different locations. One is in Gethsemane's garden, the other in the high priest's courtyard. In order better to understand Peter's behaviour, however, before looking closely at these scenes, we must use flashbacks of some earlier occurences. Rather soon in their relationship, Jesus had confided to Peter that He was, indeed, the promised Messiah. But in sharing this knowledge about Himself, Jesus revealed another secret. He identified Himself as the Suffering Servant of Israel, who was destined to suffer and die on a cross of shame. This second revelation so deeply upset Peter, that he refused to listen to any part of it. *"Heaven preserve you, Lord,"* he said to Jesus, *"this must not happen to you"* (Mt 16:22). Analysing this exclamatory prayer of Peter, it sounds as though it is coming from his Nurturing and Protective Parent. Yes. It expresses the misplaced over-protectiveness of a confirmed "Rescuer" who refused to lis-

DAY TWO : LISTENING

ten-in-faith. Jesus' response is to administer a sharp rebuke, in order to shock Peter out of his game-playing: " *Get behind me, Satan! You are an obstacle in my path, because you are thinking not as God thinks but as human beings do."* (Mt 16:23). Later happenings make it clear that Peter, the O.K. fisherman, was not listening this time either. Just as he would not listen on a number of other important occasions, when his Guru warned him not to be presumptuous :

> *Simon, Simon! Look, Satan has got his wish to sift you all like wheat... I tell you, Peter, by the time the cock crows today you will have denied three times that you know me,.. Why are you asleep? Get up and pray not to be put to the test.* (Lk 22:31,34,46)

Why did this leader of the apostolic community not listen so many times, despite the fact that he was warned of a serious crisis? Using T.A. analysis we can make an educated guess--and that's all it can be, a guess, but perhaps a valuable one.

Before his big conversion experience that came at the time of Jesus' death and resurrection, Peter's basic life-position appears to have been, "I'm O.K.; you're not O.K." His strong self-reliance was founded upon his feelings of adequacy and confidence in his own considerable resources. Faith and trusting in the Lord's grace didnot appear to enter centrally into Peter's view of life. Let us test this guess by turning now to the two episodes, in the garden and the high priest's courtyard.

In The Garden

When the police arrived to seize Jesus, a very sleepy Peter was suddenly energised into action. He reacted to the situation as a "Rescuer". No matter what the other apostles didnot do, at least he had to do something, something to "save" Jesus from this terrible plight! Peter was physically strong; he could use his sharp steel sword with deadly effect. So, Peter became a "Rescuer" of the Messiah by becoming a "Persecutor", attacking an (unarmed?) bystander, slashing off the ear of the high priest's servant. Peter's behaviour is unwanted by Jesus, unneeded and definitely unhelpful. *"Put your sword back, for all who draw the sword will die by the sword. Or do you think that I cannot appeal to my Father, who would promptly send more than twelve legions of angels to my defence? But then, how would the scriptures be fulfilled that say this is the way it must be?"* (Mt 26:52-54), It is typically Peter's "game" of being a Rescuer: impulsive, dramatic, and sadly destructive. Jesus rebukes Peter's violence--in effect, telling him that He has no need of a "Rescuer" and that what He does is done freely. Then He befriends Peter's perceived "enemy"; He touches the high priest's servant, healing the wound caused by Peter. (Lk 22:51)

In The Courtyard

Full of goodwill and generosity, yet profoundly confused, in Peter's determination to follow Jesus to the end, he remains absolutely dogged--and apparently still operating from his life- position of I'm O.K,; you're not O.K." In the high priest's compound, Peter is on "enemy" grounds. Like Samson shorn both of his hair and Nazirite gifts of power, Peter Fisher is left to his own terribly vulnerable defenses. A maid-servant, relative of the man injured by Peter, confronts him to his face, *"Didn't I see you in the garden with him?"* (Jn 18:26) Hearing this question and its implied accusation Peter moves from the "Rescuer" position in the Drama Triangle to that of "Victim". His mask of shallow assurance is ripped away. Fully hooked into an "uproar" transaction, Peter responds, *"I do not know, I do not understand what you are talking about"* (Mk 14:68). After a few minutes this same woman repeats her accusation. Peter retorts with another strong denial and adds an oath for emphasis (Mt 26:72). A little later the bystanders come up and continue the confrontation with Peter:

> *"You are certainly one of them too! Why, your accent gives you away."* Then Peter started cursing and swearing. *"I do not know the man."* (Mt 26:74-75).

Then it happened. Something very, very painful but very redemptive for Peter. Only St. Luke's account gives us this telling detail.

> *At that instant, while Peter was still speaking, the cock crowed, and the Lord turned and looked straight at*

DAY TWO : LISTENING

> Peter, and Peter remembered the Lord's words when he had said to him, "Before the cock crows today, you will have disowned me three times" (Lk 22:60-62).

It was just a gesture, a glance. It was over in a second. But with this deliberate gaze there flowed powerful love from Christ's heart. It was a life-giving communication, *an invitation to LISTEN.* It was a non-verbal call for Peter to hear not with his head but with his heart. To listen in faith and to respond wholeheartedly, acknowledging his own need for salvation, for liberation from his untruthful, unloving "games" of playing Rescuer, Persecutor and Victim ! An invitation to remember all the times he, Peter, the chosen, trusted friend, had not listened but had conveniently forgotten that he had spurned his Lord on many occasions. An invitation now to confess his games and to accept unconditional forgiveness. Luke tells us that *"Peter remembered the Lord's words.... And he went outside and wept bitterly."* (Lk. 22:62)

The tears were of disillusionment. But the moment was of truth, which Peter accepted in order to be absolved of his sin of selfrighteousness. It would seem to me that with this event Peter began to be freed from his vicious triangle of playing false roles.

Listening To Cultural Communities

In IHR we spend much time taking an honest and systematic look at our habits of listening/non-listening both to the Lord and to our sisters and brothers with whom we live and labour. We are encouraged, as well, to examine our communities. Take, for example, India's Scheduled Castes (S.C.) and Scheduled Tribes (S.T.). They number over 170 million people. These past ten years I have been honoured to live and to work closely with members of these two large cultural groups. I count many of my friends from among them During this decade I have come to realise that the centuries of oppression have left deep wounds on the S.C. and S.T. communities. Certainly not all, but very many persons of the S.C./S.T., whom I have served in IHRs and CRs, believe the false messages given them verbally and non verbally by other castes that "We're O.K.; You're not O.K.". Conditioned by constant propaganda day

A TIME FOR HEALING

and night, especially in India's lakhs of villages, S.C./S.T. have introjected upon themselves the negative prejudices of casteism. As a result those of S.C./S.T. backgrounds perceive themselves as "Victims" within the Drama Traingle. (Note : We have to be very clear about with what topic we're dealing. Over centuries, perhaps even millenia, there has been a terrible victimisation of these oppressed communities. As a result of this historically verified oppression, our hypothesis is that many S.C./S.T. have interiorised their inhuman social situation into a psychological, emotional and spiritual state. This seems to me to be almost inevitable, given their sad history. But these facts also challenge S.C./S.T to be healed and liberated. I deeply believe that Christ invites India's S.C./S.T. communities to be freed from all oppression--social, economic, political and religious. I believe that Christ promises all peoples, including S.C./S.T., authentic freedom (see Jn 8:36; Ga 5:1; Rm 6:15, etc.). The hope that comes from this promise constitutes the most powerful motivation for S.C./S.T. to become Christ's disciples in order for them to hear Him say, *If the Son sets you free, you will indeed be free."* This deep desire for authentic, permanent liberation accounts for the fact that of all communities in India these two have been for over a century the most receptive to the Good News. Nor is it any surprise that together they make up over 70% of Indian Christians. I believe that this process of real liberation begins with a core experience, within their minds, hearts, and souls. It starts with a faithvision of who they are in God's heart. IHRs offer Christians of Scheduled Caste and Tribe backgrounds such a spiritual experience. For this reason I and my associates have looked upon this IHR ministry to be a catechumenate of faith-renewal.

No matter what our ethnic background may be, during an IHR we examine whether we are really listening to the S.C./S.T. communities and responding to them as Christ would have us.

We honestly ask ourselves whether social prejudices have influenced us, whether we sometimes play "Persecutor" and "Rescuer" in our relating with S.C./S.T. If we have been graced by God as to be born into either one of these two communities, part of our self-evanagelisation is to be freed from all "games".

Sharing/Listening

This third general reflection ends with partner sharing, choosing one or the other from these suggested topics:

(1) Tell your partner what your own basic life-position is now and how it affects your listening patterns--with yourself, God and others.

(2) How did you get your first name? Do you like it? What does it mean linguistically? What does it mean to you personally? Have you also a nickname? If so, share how you received it and what it means to you.

(3) Do you identify with Peter Fisher in any way? Share this and other insights that you have received during this session.

(4) What is your way of relating with those of S.C./S.T. communities? Can you verify from your own experience that listening to them "game-free" is a challenge to you? Give your reasons.

Conlcude the session with prayer, partners praying for each other and for the whole retreat group, petitioning the grace of being able to listen-in-faith to God, to self and to others.

* **Eucharistic Celebration :** The Mass for Special Occasions (Pastoral and Spiritual Meetings) is suggested, along with the second eucharistic prayer. Readings : 1) Ac 2:42-47; 2) Ps 95 with a response from verse 7: " *If only you would listen to him today!"*; 3) Lk 2:41-52a. The theme is listening-in-faith- together. The Holy Family is our model. Jesus, Mary and Joseph as one family experienced the same temple celebration, but not all members received the same message from the Spirit. God's Word is multi-valiant ! The challenge to listen not only to God but to each other's unique experience of God is here underlined.

* **Night Common Sharing :** This nightly exercise in community building enables us each for ourselves to witness to the lights and shadows of our retreat's second day. We are one pilgrim community, but we are as individuals very different. This fact is demonstrated as each retreatant reviews the "inside story" of their own day's journey.

* Team Evaluation : The team discerns together what the Lord is saying to the community. This listening is done in a spirit of prayer and openness. If confidentiality is demanded of each retreatant, it is more than ever required of staff members. Since retreatants are encouraged to sign their names for one-to- one guidance, and this list is on the bulletin board, there is no violation of confidence for the staff to keep track on who is and who is not going for personal direction and inner healing prayer. In this way the staff helps discern how effective the retreat is; for, one-to-one is practically irreplaceable to have deeper healing.

PRAYER FOR THE GRACE TO LISTEN
(For Day Two)

Abba, Father, You have gifted me with wondrous baptismal faith/
To hear the inaudible, to see the invisible/
To ponder Your Word, to walk Your ways/
Too deep for me to think, too high for me to reach/
To wait on You and Your children with patient respect/
Knowing that self-gift is on the other's terms, not only mine/
Jesus, I need You to walk by and call me within myself/
Past inner layers of fears, untruth, habits of make-believe/
Painful though it be, Lord, glance straight at me/
As you did with Peter, stir up heavy memories of days and nights/
When I didn't give ear or heart to cries inside and out/Yes, Lord,
Say to me, too: "You of so little faith, why doubt?"/
Open my mind, Lord, to listen to You, God's Word/
In scriptures and signs of life's happenings around/
Spirit, clean my disciple's ears each morn anew/
As when first I was born through You to love and listening/
Ephphatha ! Be opened again my soul to hear God's voice/
Within the cave of my heart let me cry out with You, *"Abba!"*/
Let leap forth a stream of living water, so I may thirsty drink/
Say to me, let me hear Your call, "Come to the Father!"

DAY THREE

A TIME FOR HEALING : BY WONDERING

How rich and deep are the wisdom and kingdom of God! Everything there is comes from him and is caused by him and exists for him. To him be glory forever! Amen.
(Rm. 11 : 33, 36)

* **AIM OF THE DAY :** (a) To admire the mysteries of creation; (b) to discover in wonder how special and sacred is each and every human being.

* **MORNING PRAYER :** Psalm 8 *("Yahweh our Lord, how majestic is your name throughout the world!")*. As we pray and reflect on this divinely motivated song, we are invited by God's Spirit to experience a sense of wonderment, praise and thanks to God for the gift of creation. Each of us is designed and desired by the Father! Without exception we are each the artistry of His love - unique unrepeatable reflections of His Word. This morning's psalm--song may be chanted or recited. A combination may be used, first recite it for comprehension and then sing it for celebration with both head and heart. In an IHR we desire to grow in appreciation of both divine and human mysteries. In this sense a "mystery" is not something simply unable to be understood. It is a reality so rich and full that our small human minds can never fully comprehend it. Problems we can *solve* but mysteries we can only *accept*--in wonder and humble gratitude. Next to the mystery of God comes the mystery of a human person, made *"little less than a god"*, crowned with *"glory and beauty"*. These two greatest mysteries are combined in one human being, Jesus, Son of God, Son of Mary. Focussing on Him we cannot but be led into a deeper sense of God's goodness and love. In this the Church encourages us:

> *In reality it is only in the mystery of the Word made flesh that the mystery of human beings truly becomes clear.*

A TIME FOR HEALING

> *For Adam, the first man, was a type of Him who was to come, Christ the Lord, Christ the new Adam, in the very revelation of the mystery of the Father and of His love, fully reveals the human person to him/herself and brings to light his/her most high calling.* (Vatican II, Pastoral Constitution On The Church In The Modern World, 22)

* **MEDITATION :** The animator spends a few minutes helping retreatants relax physically in order to enter into the healing presence of the Eucharistic Lord. Starting with the top of the head and slowly moving through each limb and organ, the retreatants are invited to call upon Christ to let His most precious Blood flow through their fatigued, sick and aching parts. We want to experience His gentle touch, as we intercede for this retreat community. The animator may wish to offer for meditation either psalm 8, which was used in Morning Prayer, or some other scriptural passage related to our day's theme of WONDER. The hymn *"Lord Make Me An Instrument Of Worship"* is proposed for an opening song. It invites retreatants to let the lyrics resound in their hearts throughout the whole day. We want to believe and to experience the Father fashioning us now, creating us constantly, building us up towards that fullness which He promises us in Christ.

* **COMMON REFLECTION I:** In an IHR we strive to discover more deeply our true identities. Strange as it may seem, many people either don't know or like who they are! They may have much information about all sorts of things. They may have remarkable skills and wide experience. But ask them the basic question, "Who are you?" They will either ask you in return, "What do you mean, Who am I?", or they will tell you some superficial facts about themselves, which you already know. What sets them apart from every other human being, what makes them a unique creature, of this they do not seem to have a clue. Ask them, "What do you most like about yourself?" They may not take you seriously or they may even tell you about their faults! Often in groups I have asked people to list their main strengths and weaknesses. Guess which list is longer? The weakness list is sometimes twice as long as the other. Many of us do not love and appreciate ourselves as the Lord tells

DAY THREE : WONDERING

us *("Love your neighbour as YOURSELF!")*. We need God's Word to teach us who we are and how to value ourselves. We need to go to our wonderful Maker to discover our preciousness.

Our Family Of Origin: Genesis 1-2

If we read the opening two chapters of the Book of Genesis prayerfully and preferably aloud, we are in for a nice surprise. Within these 56 verses there is a sense of mystery and wonderment, a kind of epic grandeur. In the background is the magnificient theme-song of creation: Love-Sharing-Itself. This love story reaches a climax in its masterwork, the first human beings. The inspired writer uses many delightful expressions in order to bring this mystery a little closer to our minds and hearts. At close of each day God is portrayed as an artist, who steps back and reviews his labour. For the first five days' work, the evening estimate a refrain, *"God saw that it was GOOD."* Here is satisfaction and pleasure in a work well done. After fashioning the first human couple on the sixth day, however, God's appraisal is different. *"God saw all he had made, and indeed it was VERY GOOD."* (Gn 1 : 31) Does it not put balm on our hearts to hear of God's delight over us!

Or are we already discounting this revelation, by saying that Adam and Eve were indeed masterpieces, whereas we are "just ordinary?" It is on divine authority through the sacred writers of the Bible that ALL human beings are shaped in God's divine image. If we do not see the beauty, maybe we do not look deeply enough:

> *What are human beings that you spare a thought for them, or the child of Adam that you care for him? Yet you have made him little less than a god* . . .*(Ps 8)*

Returning to the Book of our origins, we pay attention to the description of Adam and Eve. The scenes are most delicately painted. Earlier Adam is shown surrounded by all sorts of animals and birds -- he is director of the most magnificent open zoo! As wonderful as these beasts may be, Adam is incomplete and lonely. *"But no helper suitable for the man was found for him"* (Gn 2 : 20).

A TIME FOR HEALING

So, with rich symbolism Yahweh is portrayed as putting Adam to sleep, removing a rib from his side, and with its help forming the first woman. God presents this final, crowning work of creation to Adam for approval. His response is the human race's first recorded love-song:

> *This one at last is bone of my bones and flesh of my flesh! She is to be called Woman, because she is taken from Man.* (Gn 2 : 23).

Adam is delighted. In Eve's face he sees God's own joyful light. Her spiritual quickness matches his own; and yet, she is so attractively different! Another person: to share and reflect his wonder and worship. Someone to understand and to be understood by and affirmed. An equal, a pilgrim partner. Rejoicing in each other at that first meeting, their grateful praise echoes throughout eternity: *"Yahweh, you have crowned us with glory and beauty, how majestic your name throughout the world!"*

A Renewed Invitation To Fullness

This harmony and melody of our planet earth's first human inhabitants after a while turned sour and flat. Instead of compliments Adam had complaints and criticism for his first friend. The tragic story related in Genesis Three, however, isn't the final word. God is too Good for that. His glory-plan for the whole human family got back "on track" with creation of a New Adam, Jesus, born through the Spirit's power of Mary, bone of her bone and flesh of her flesh. This new Model has been gifted to us as our Way, Truth and Life, to lead us unto our Father's own fullness:

> *In him, in bodily form, lives divinity in all its fullness, and in him you too find your own fulfilment........You have been buried with him by your baptism; by which, too, you have been raised up with him through your belief in the power of God who raised him from the dead.*
>
> (Col 2 : 9, 12)

DAY THREE : WONDERING

Jesus teaches us to trust, to listen, to wonder, and to co-operate as mature persons with this movement towards a new creation, the fullness of God's Reign. Our Lord challenges us, therefore, to let go of all our negative, pessimistic, unproductive ways. We learned these destructive habits from the Old Adam. Many of us have modelled ourselves upon bad-news messages. The New Adam, however, invites us to hear and to live by his Good News: we are being uninterruptedly invited--and empowered--to work with the Spirit's movement to establish God's Reign, which is a glory-plan for the whole human family. People are called not only to have more but to be more. Whether we believe this or not is indicated how we inter-relate with people. We can also discover indications of our rock-bottom value system by looking at the way we use our time. T.A. offers us two instruments to do this, the "Stroke-O-Gram" and "Time-O-Gram".

From The Psychological Plane To The Spiritual

Before seeing what these graphs look like, let us repeat for emphasis an important principle that we use throughout IHRs. It is this: psychology and other behavioural sciences can often help us find within our lives real obstacles to healthy living. Using these sciences we can identify and give names to our illnesses. These hindrances very often are root causes for spiritual weaknesses. The reverse is also true: original sin along with our personal sins can and do have physical, mental and emotional repercussions. We can trace back the whole course of our brokenness. Starting with the physical-psychological phenomena we can follow them back to their spiritual causes. We are one integrated mystery, we are inspirited bodies and bodily spirits. Our re-creation in Christ by baptism is a *new beginning* towards a plentitude of life. This fullness will become a reality only in heaven when we shall enjoy communion with our Triune God and God's children. In light of our destiny and with a determination to grow towards God's gift of fullness let's now see these two paragraphs.

A TIME FOR HEALING

Graphing How We Relate And Spend Our Time

Here are the two devices TA gives to help us become aware how we and others in our families have inter-related and how, as a result, we have chosen certain patterns for use of time. The STROKE-O-GRAM has as its unit of measure, a single social transaction, within a 24 hour period. These are divided into five types: (a) unconditional positive strokes, (b) conditional positive strokes, (c) unconditional negative strokes, (d) conditional negative strokes, and (e) no strokes. In the Stroke-O-Gram below, the score at end of a day reads: UPS, self=2, others=6; CPS, nil; UNS, self=2, others=0; CNS, nil. NS, self=5, others, 4.

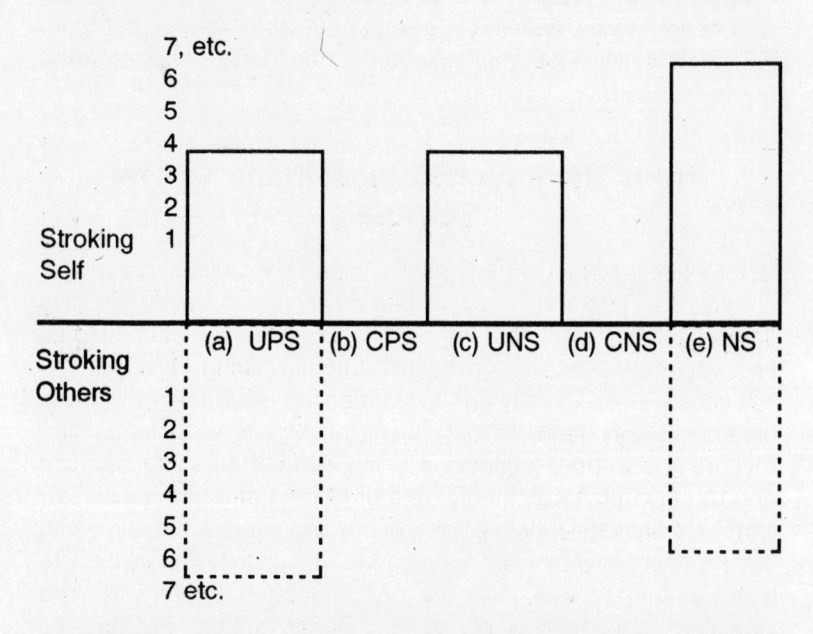

```
                7, etc.
                6
                5
                4
                3
                2
Stroking        1
Self
                ┌───────┐           ┌───────┐           ┌───────┐
                │ (a)UPS│ (b)CPS    │(c)UNS │ (d)CNS    │(e) NS │
Stroking        │       │           │       │           │       │
Others      1   │       │           │       │           │       │
            2   │       │           │       │           │       │
            3   │       │           │       │           │       │
            4   │       │           │       │           │       │
            5   │       │           │       │           │       │
            6   └───────┘           │       │           └───────┘
            7 etc.
```

The TIME-O-GRAM has as its unit of measure, hours per day. There are six divisions: (a) Intimacy, (b) Withdrawal, (c) Rituals, (d) Activities, (e) Pastimes, and (f) Games. In the graph below for one day the score: Intimacy, nil; Withdrawal, self=1, others=2; Rituals, self=2, others=1; Activities, self=1, others=8; Pastimes, self=8, others=1; Games, nil.

DAY THREE : WONDERING

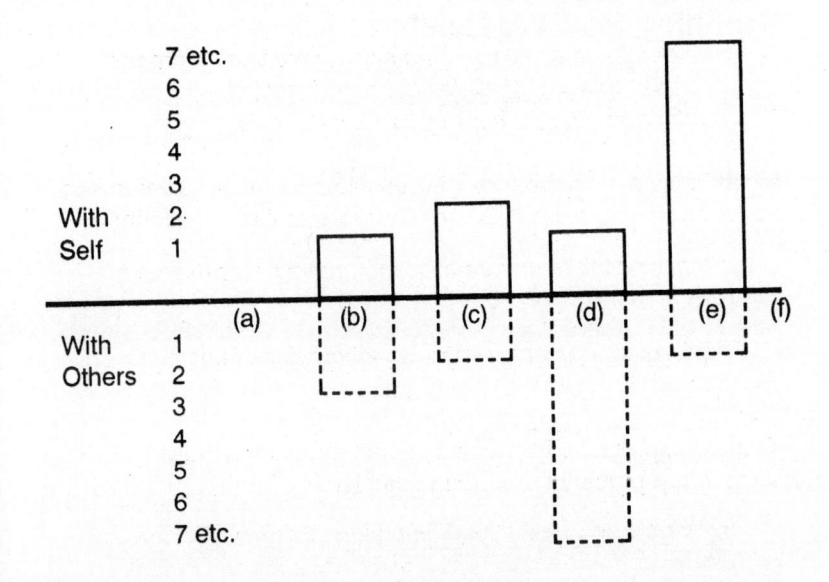

```
         7 etc.
         6
         5
         4
         3
With     2
Self     1
           (a)   (b)   (c)   (d)   (e)   (f)
With     1
Others   2
         3
         4
         5
         6
         7 etc.
```

The purpose of the Stroke-O-Gram is to help us to realise through use of a graph how many times and with what kind of recognition we have/have not appreciated others and ourselves in community. The unit of measure is a single social transaction over a 24 hour day period (or **week, month**). It's essential to note that in themselves none of the five kind of strokes has a moral value. Depending upon the relationship and circumstances each may be good, appropriate, loving; and each may be bad, unloving, inappropriate. Different folks need different strokes at different times, as Dr. Muriel James points out in her inspiring book *Born To Love*.

An Explanation Of Stroke Types

We now briefly look at each of the five kinds of stroking.

(a) *Unconditional Positive Strokes* (UPS): These affirm the other person/s for whom they are and for what they have done. Communicated with truth-in-love, an UPS encourages the other to grow. A perfect example is God's consolation for His children:

> *I have called you by your name, you are mine....I regard you as precious.... you are honoured and I love you....Do not be afraid for I am with you* (Is 43:1, 4-5)

No other kind of stroke so builds up or restores interpersonal relationships as do UPS. Some other examples from scripture:

> ** You are salt for the earth....You are light for the world.* (Mt 5:13-14)

> ** There, truly, is an Israelite in whom there is no deception.* (Jn 1:47)

Some people use UPS in an easy manner; such strokes create a very friendly atmosphere. Some samples:

* "You did exactly the right thing. Congrats!"
* "You're correct again, as usual!"
* "You look wonderful! I wish I knew the secret of your good health?"
* "You have the ability of putting people at their ease."

(b) *Conditional Positive Strokes* (CPS: What makes this transaction different from the UPS is a restriction or provision. In other words, in place of an unlimited, open acceptance, there is a condition laid down. This may be for reasons of etiquette, personal taste, accepted conventions, or moral law. Here are a few instances:

* "You are most welcome; but, first, kindly remove your footwear before entering the house."
* "You are free to sit anywhere you please, but kindly refrain from smoking."
* "If you wish to remain a member of this association, you must pay your monthly fee."

DAY THREE : WONDERING

(c) *Unconditional Negative Strokes* (UNS): Verbally or non-verbally, this is strong language. The UNS may be a painful transaction that sets down boundaries like demarcations between people. These may be temporary or permanent, based upon social, cultural or religious values.

* "Alas for you, Scribes and Pharisees, you hypocrites! You clean the outside of cup and dish and leave the inside full of extortion and intemperance. Blind Pharisee!" (Mt 23:25)

* "This behaviour is entirely unacceptable here. Leave the room."

* "In this game there is to be no arguing with the umpire. You must depart from the field at once."

(d) *Conditional Negative Strokes* (CNS): The CNS communicates the same message as a CPS but in more emphatic terms, because there is a prohibition.

* "No one is welcomed here as long as he/she does not remove their footware before entering."

* "No one is to sit in this room as long as they are smoking."

* "No one may remain a club member unless they pay the monthly fees."

(e) *No Strokes* (NS): We have learned from experiments that infants and small children literally cannot survive or grow normally without a minimum of physical stroking--the loving touch of a mother, a hug, pat on the head, an embrace or kiss. So, too, older people do not grow into healthy, holy persons without social attention, recognition and encouragement. This is so essential for human maturity that both children and adults prefer even negative strokes to no strokes at all. For this reason solitary confinement, whether in jail, family or community, is the most intense kind of punishment. In such social isolation many persons quickly get sick, go insane or else die. For, God made us to live in a society of love.

Spending Our Time To Get Some Positive Strokes

An indication as to whether we appreciate and correctly value ourselves and others is the way we use our time. Teaching us something important about the mystery of human motivation, T.A. tells us that we spend time in six ways. Why? *In order to get the strokes we want.* For, just as there are stimulus-hunger and recognition-hunger, there is also a hunger for time-structuring. We have a felt need to programme our time. We seek the rewards of certain kinds of recognition that comes from each category: (a) intimacy, (b) withdrawal, (c) rituals, (d) activities, (e) pastimes, and (f) games. The subject of time-structuring is certainly culturally conditioned. Accordingly, there will be some different classifications under these six headings. Besides, T.A. experts have their own definitions, depending upon their experience and value systems. Our own working descriptions are as follows:

(a) *Intimacy:* This is between two persons, or among a number of people in which the truth is lived in love (Ep 4:15). In intimacy there is unconditional acceptance of the other/s. This does not mean necessarily there is agreement about everything. But there is a bond of faithfulness and compassion in which persons are free to be themselves--"warts and all"--free to grow and change at their own pace. Intimacy means a relationship that is open and non-possessive. It affirms, supports, and enriches the other/s. There is no fear of being rejected. So, there is no need to wear masks in pretence. We see intimacy in Jesus' communicating with the twelve apostles, particularly just before the passion (see Jn 13-17). We hear it described in Acts 2:46; 4:32-35. To create intimacy within a community there must be a sense of basic equality and mutuality. People will find intimacy difficult, if they are afraid to trust others with a knowledge of their own inner thoughts, feelings, strengths and weaknesses. Defensive and "gamey" people will also find intimacy impossible. Intimacy's ADVANTAGES: limitless! Its

DAY THREE : WONDERING

DANGERS: that it takes the other/s for granted. In order words, the dangers of intimacy are those of all human love on this earth. It needs continual purification and discernment. When our pilgrim existence is completed, we will enjoy for all eternity a life of perfect intimacy. We shall know and be known as God knows us.

(b) *Withdrawal:* It can be physical or psychological. It can be healthy or unhealthy. ADVANTAGES: it can afford relaxation and much needed rest for future creative work. DANGERS: if it is motivated from "bad feelings", it can lead to stroke- starvation. In this sense, its extreme form is suicide--slow or fast, accidental or deliberate. We may assume from the gospel accounts that long before he withdrew physically to take his own life, Judas had withdrawn from the apostolic community both psychologically and spiritually.

(c) *Rituals:* They are almost completely predictable interactions having set patterns. They become habitual. Many customs and good manners come under this heading. There are rituals sacred and profane, cultural individual. It is fascinating, for example, to see the variety of symbolism used in rituals of greeting and of taking leave within different cultures and even within different families of the same cultural community. Bihar's Santhal Tribal Community has over a dozen ways of greeting through non-verbal ritual gestures before any word is spoken. This ritual changes depending upon the kinship relationship. Sub-cultures within any large community are recognised by their different set of social rituals. ADVANTAGES: we fulfill many of our obligations through Rituals, with a minimum of fussing and loss of time. DANGERS: Rituals can easily become depersonalised and lose their meaning.

(d) *Activities:* These are projects, transactions dealing with definite data or set sequences, e.g. work skills. ADVANTAGES: they can be productive, creative, useful and rewarding. DANGERS: "workaholics" are people who lose themselves in their routines, neglecting interpersonal contacts and making intimacy impossible.

(e) *Pastimes:* In Activities our way of using time is usually very structured by prescribed methods in order to produce results, whereas in Pastimes we are relaxed, recreating ourselves with the joy of involvement, e.g. watching nature, gardening, sightseeing, reading a newspaper or magazine for relaxation. Pastimes may be verbal or non-verbal, creative or stagnant, healthy or unhealthy. ADVANTAGES: we can be relaxed, relieved from the pressures of work. Unlike professional Activities, in Pastimes we can select our companions, the time and place of our recreation. DANGERS: Pastimes can be excuses for avoiding duties of work and social commitments. Like vacations, healthy Pastimes presume work done in the past and work to be done in the future. If too much time is devoted to Pastimes, maybe it's time to review our motivations and priorities.

(f) *Games:* These are ulterior (double-level) social transactions, which end up with all "players" hurting from bad feelings generated by these untruthful ways of relating. ADVANTAGES: there aren't any honest advantages. They are basically dishonest ways of relating with others. People usually learn "games" very early in life as children, in order to survive in painful, dysfunctional situations. Unless effectively confronted, gamey children as adults usually continue their destructive patterns in order to get and give negative strokes. This means they are in not-O.K. life-positions and have learned to seek negative strokes rather than endure a life of no-strokes. DANGERS: being untruthful and unloving transactions, games are hurtful to everyone concerned. They are often unconscious, addictive, habitual and destructive. By formula games end with a "pay- off" of bad-feelings and diminished trust in all players.

Sharing Exercises For All Three Reflections

* COMMON REFLECTIONS II-III: After explanations and a few demonstrations of the Stroke-O-Gram (SOG) and Time-O-Gram (TOG), retreatants spend their time in doing their own graphs and sharing them with their partners. The following exercises will take

DAY THREE : WONDERING

more time than most sessions afford; it will be profitable "homework" during your leisure time of the retreat.

(1) A principle of T.A. is that we stroke others as we ourselves have been stroked in childhood. This general rule holds good until and unless we become aware of these patterns and make free decisions to change them. Make a SOG of your early childhood of strokes you remember yourself to have most often received from one or both of your parents. After presenting this SOG to your partner/s, share your thoughts and feelings.

(2) Do your own SOG for today, i.e. how you presently inter-relate with others in your community. Compare this adult SOG with your childhood SOG done in the first exercise. Do you see any connection? Share your discoveries with others.

(3) Do your present day TOG. Share this with your partner.

(4) Relate your SOG and TOG with your perceived basic life position, along with the typical game-role which you find yourself playing most often (Rescuer, Victim, Oppressor).

(5) Relate all this to your relationship with God, your appreciation of self and others.

* HOLY HOUR: The animator helps retreatants centre on the Lord Who is present sacramentally. This divine presence is ACTIVE. As Lord and Saviour Jesus does not "just sit there" under the appearance of bread. He is inviting and empowering us. He listens and speaks to those with living faith. A basic principle of IHRs is that the Lord calls us by name to be responsible to God, to ourselves and others, to be responsible for our unique mission for promoting God's reign. At this stage of our retreat there is a tendency in some people to become introverted-- in an unhealthy sense. During each Holy Hour we are challenged to be still. To look and to listen unto the Lord. We are also given a precious chance to speak. This is not self-talk. We speak to Him on behalf of our own needs for healing and those of others. This is a moment of grace allowing us to be intimate with the Lord, open to Him Who beckons us to be His honest friends and committed partners for building a new creation not only for all peoples but for our wounded, abused planet earth.

* EUCHARISTIC CELEBRATION: A votive Mass of Our Lady is recommended, with the first eucharistic prayer for young people. Readings are thematised on Mary's growing sense of wonder and adoration as she realises by faith-stages that her Creator is continually inviting her as His partner in the new act of creation, the redemption, sanctification and transformation of the human family. Suggested readings: 1) Pr 8:22-31, or Is 9:1- 6, or Is 61:10-11; 2) Psalm meditation from 1 S 2:1, 4-8 with the responsorial verse, "My heart exults in the Lord my Saviour"; 3) Lk 1: 46-55.

* NIGHT COMMON SHARING: As the group becomes more confident with itself, especially during this time of common sharing some individuals will tend to "talk too much". The animator does well to intervene crisply in order to keep the sharing dispersed. In this way everyone who wishes will have a chance to contribute. The SOG and TOG can reveal previously hidden areas of brokenness and need for healing. The truth can, at times, shock us. A healthy, holy sense of astonishment may turn into numbing bewilderment. The staff will monitor to recognise such developments, lest too much revelation come too soon. This would do more harm than good. A sensitive leadership, therefore, is alert to offer support to those who start showing signs of "over-exposure".

* TEAM EVALUATION: In IHR , one of the real dangers of using psychological instruments--concepts, methods, exercises--is that prayerfulness is lost and a heady seminar atmosphere replaces it. This results in a loss of central focus. Then our own thinking and feelings become more important than the Lord's action within us and other members of the retreat community. Balance of both content and time investment is needed to ensure that a proper retreat mood always is maintained.

DAY THREE : WONDERING

PRAYER FOR THE GRACE TO WONDER
(For Day Three)

Abba, wonderful You are in all Your works/
Too many blessings for me to count in one lifespan/
Despite the ugly ruins our pride and power have built/
I see Your beauty peeking out of garbage heaps and human tragedies/
You delight me, invite me to raise my arms to You in thanks/
Hidden Love, You mother me with new surprises ev'ryday/
Jesus, gentle poor man. songster. eyes and hearts You're opening/
Rejoicing in flower fields and birds tree-nesting/
Most of all to be in our midst delighting/
Helping my heavy spirit get off the ground for praising/
Spirit, Light within, You waken me to see God's glory-plan/
You nudge me--at times You shove me--to marvel mysteries/
To rest in awe as the jigsaw puzzle pieces of His design/
Fall into place with disconcerting, unprogrammed pace.

DAY FOUR

A TIME FOR HEALING : BY REMEMBERING

> Can a woman forget her baby at the breast, feel no pity for the child she has borne? Even if these were to forget, I shall not forget you. Look, I have engraved you on the palms of my hands.
>
> (Is 49:15-16)

* AIM OF THE DAY: (a) To share our personal histories; and (b) to discover that the Lord heals wounded memories, thus freeing us to say to life today our own full "Yes!"

* MORNING PRAYER: *Psalm 139 ("Yahweh, you examine me and know me ......").* Our whole personal history--from the first moment of life within our mothers till our final breath--is in the Lord's hand. To God there is no past nor future. A distinctive part of every IHR is recalling wounded "root" memories. These are like precious, hidden artifacts which anthropologists must dig for and discover, because they are buried many layers beneath the surface. Root memories mark our lives indelibly. They are sources of much pain and confusion; they are also keys to understanding our lives and personalities. During this retreat we want to discover some of these influential wounded recollections. We desire to give them to the Lord in order that He Who examines and knows us may make us whole and beautiful, as we are designed to be in the Father's heart. we realise that inner healing, like redemption and life itself, is a long process. But we want *to experience* that we are in fact on the Lord's "recovery road". Only then shall we be able to contribute our talents in loving service, like a melodious voice in the choir of God's children and of all creation.

Many people enter the IHR burdened and heavy with "unredeemed memories". Such folks are bitter, complaining, pessimistic. In this

DAY FOUR : REMEMBERING

state they cannot appreciate or wholeheartedly join the Church as she celebrates her eucharistic memories *"about the marvels of God"* (Ac 2:12)--the Father's creation, the Son's redemption, and the Spirit's work of sanctifying transformation. These peak movements cannot "get through" to people who are burdened with unhealed root memories because they are blocked inside. To make the situation still more difficult, many IHR participants are not aware whence their misery comes from. Such is our human situation! God's greatest gifts, Jesus and the Spirit, are not the conscious centre of our lives. For these wounded people the Church's great memorial becomes an empty ritual, a time of distracting pain, an anxious preoccupation with themselves. The main aim of this fourth day is systematically to review our personal family of origin in order to discover our graces and our wounds so that we may bring them earnestly to our Saviour. With Christ's Body we want to be able to recall all that Jesus said and did for us. He is the reason of our confidence. On the day when we have begun consciously to experience that our broken memories are being healed, that will be for us the "Lord's Day". It will be the first day of the rest of our lives. We will then be able to proclaim Christ's redemption to others from our own inner experience, *"what we have seen and heard"* (Ac 4:21).

* MEDITATION: The Holy Spirit is the "Great Reminder" (see Jn 14:26). This "Other Paraclete" is sent within us as Supreme Gift of both the Father and of Jesus, their Personified Love. The Spirit helps us remember God's great deeds of the past so that we may recognise the Lord's saving presence today. Psalm 139 is suggested; special attention is paid to verses 13-18. Applied to our lives we want to realise what these inspired words mean for us.

* COMMON REFLECTION I: As usual the first business is to review our morning meditation. The animator invites retreatants to share with the group how they are/are not praying. This daily review is educative and healing. Many of us, for mysterious reasons, assume that we are the only ones in the world who have difficulties praying. Through this open exchange we learn that meditation is rarely a glorious Mount Tabor experience. More often it is like

A TIME FOR HEALING

Jacob's dark, isolated and painful wrestling match with God (see Gn 32:23-33).

Today's Problems Rooted In Yesterday's Wounds

We want to discover that quite a few--though certainly not all-- of our problems as adults have their root causes in early childhood. Here are a couple of actual examples.

(1) Fat John And Skinny Alex:

> John is a very successful, top officer in one of India's most famous companies. To look at, he is heavyset, in fact overweight. He likes to eat plentifully and he also expects his house guests to eat as amply as he. Whenever his friend Alex visits him for supper, John insists on filling Alex's plate to overflowing. This brings a complaint from his friend, "John, I can't eat all that food! Whenever I see so much in front of me I actually feel sick in my stomach." This criticism falls on deaf ears, because everytime John makes a joke of it. "You're so thin, Alex! I want to help put some flesh on you."

COMMENT: There is an interesting history behind this recurring incident. When John was small, there was a famine in his part of the country. For a long time food was not easily available. On top of this, John was sickly. So his mother took extra care that her son John was given special dishes to build him up. This extra food could be given to John because other members of the family made real sacrifices, particularly his mother. But young John learned to hate this extra food. He longed to eat what everyone else in the family had; because of his poor health this was denied him. Such was the strange, contradictory way John grew up.

Alex was from a very poor family. As a boy he was "thin as a toothpick" and he kept thin his whole life. His mother's health had always been delicate. She picked and chose her food carefully and taught Alex to do the same. At school Alex was given a nickname by other boys. "Skinny"--because he looked so starved. Due to the family's poverty Alex had to give up studies and earn his living early in life. In IHR he introduced himself as the least educated of the whole group. Yet, it was soon clear that when questions were asked, Alex's hand was always the first to be raised for an answer. He gave an image of himself as a real "know-it-all". His clothes were tip-top, fashionable and expensive. One day Alex was confronted with this apparent contradiction: why did he insist on playing an intellectual show-off, while at the same time publicising his lack of formal education? And why did he wear very stylish clothes despite the fact that his income was modest? To both discrepancies Alex owned up and said that he did not understand himself.

A T.A. Overview Of John And Alex

Before describing how John and his friend Alex found healing, a clarification is needed. Now a few people in IHR misunderstand why we review our early parental relationships. These folks are very conscientious and affectionate. They consider analysis of parent-child memories as falsely judging our elders. To them, evaluation of mothers and fathers by their grown children is disrespectful ingratitude. "They did the best they could do!" they say defensively. This is true. "We can never repay our debt to parents for the gift of life and nurturing", they add. This also is true. But both facts are beside the point. In no way do we internally judge our parents or blame them for our limitations. Actually we engage in these family-of-origin reflections precisely *in order to love and appreciate our parents more!* A typical IHR begins with renewal of this most basic relationship, parent-child. Once reconciled with our parents, we can also experience wonderful renewal with the Trinitarian Community and with everyone else. This is the first point to have clearly in mind.

Point two: in tracing back to root memories we are not dealing with our actual parents, neither as they were, nor as they are today--whether they are alive on earth with us or alive with the Lord in eternity. In root memory work we are dealing with our parents *as*

A TIME FOR HEALING

we remember them. Our early recollections of our parents are *always distorted perceptions both positively and negatively.* Now all this may sound like playing with words, but it is not. As a famous philosopher-humourist once remarked, rather late in life we learn that most of our problems have been only in our heads! There have been and are today parents who are neglectful and abusive of their children. In IHR we do not judge them. We face up to a triple duty: (1) being responsible for ourselves; (2) being responsible for our changed perceptions of reality, as we understand it, and then (3) getting on with fulfillment of our life's mission. Now, back to John and Alex.

Both of these two men as adults were playing "games". Let's use T.A. insights to analyse their personalities. Then we shall relate this data to John and Alex. According to T.A. there are five stages in personality formation:

(1)	(2)	(3)	(4)	(5)
Early STROKING experienced childhood & its resulting messages	Early DECISIONS based on stroking messages	Early LIFE POSITION based on these child decisions	Early MAIN ROLE & LIFE-SCRIPT choices	ACTING OUT the drama & confirming it by daily experience

(1) EARLY STROKING: Starting from its earliest memories--during the nine months' gestation--a child senses intuitively either it is loved and accepted for itself or that it is not. This perception is based upon maternal "stroking", that is, the kind of recognition it receives from its mother and significant others. This stroking is physical/psychological, verbal/non- verbal, positive/negative. For survival, stroking is needed by all humans. Childhood "messages" are the child's own interpretations of the strokes--their meaning. These interpretations may be accurate or inaccurate. The important point to note is that *they are the child's interpretation, not the parents'.* For example, a child may be deeply wanted by its mother. Despite her best efforts, however, the child may interpret its

mother's strokes negatively and falsely perceive itself as unwanted. Again, return to the actual histories of John and Alex. When John was a child, his mother stroked him positively, wanting to show him that he was her favourite. John, however, mistakenly interpreted these acts of loving sacrifice; he perceived himself as being unjustly punished, as segregated from his brothers and sisters. Young Alex was also stroked positively by his mother in childhood. He received two messages from his mother. First, "I love you and so I teach you to be very careful about what you eat." Secondly, "I am sick and poor; I want you to discontinue your education in order to support me and the family." Both of these perceived communications seemed reasonable at the time Alex was still a boy. But a child unconsciously often distorts what it hears. Verbal and non-verbal precepts are unknowingly turned around into negative equivalents. These can become extremely demanding--and demeaning--injunctions. While still very young, Alex translated his mother's two messages in this way: "Never eat well or become well-built!" "Never be well-educated, otherwise you will not be doing your duty to your family or to me!" Alex was not happy about these injunctions but they were messages which played inside his adult mind constantly.

(2) EARLY DECISIONS: Depending upon the quality and quantity of strokes together with their interpretations, a child will put "two-and-two" together about itself in relation to its family. This can happen as early as the end of its first year. Unconsciously the child decides that it is loved, wanted, accepted, and that its parents are happy with it. Or, the child will decide that it is not loved by its parents and other family members. This decision may be changed in early childhood. On the basis of messages they received during meal time while they were still very young, both John and Alex decided they were not loved or accepted.

(3) EARLY LIFE-POSITION: Perhaps already by end of the third year each child has unconsciously chosen a psychological position along with feelings for and orientation towards itself and others. This is called a "life-position". It will be initially a hesitant stance, but after some testing, it will be confirmed by the child's own filtered

A TIME FOR HEALING

experiences. The typical position in early childhood is, "I'm not O.K., but you big folks are O.K." This is the feeling perspective of a tiny child. It is also the position of adults who make superficial comparisons with others and find themselves wanting. This position later can become "I'm not O.K., and you're not O.K. either!"

The position "I'am O.K., you're O.K." is healthy and open. *This does not mean agreement on all issues but acceptance of persons as they are.* We can have no doubt this was the childhood stance of Jesus and of those happy children nurtured in totally loving households.

While their mothers love them and made many sacrifices for them, both John and Alex in early childhood chose the negative position, "I'm not O.K."

(4) **EARLY CHOICES OF MAIN ROLE AND LIFE-SCRIPT:** Unconsciously trying to cope with people around it, upon whom it depends for life, the small child will next choose a predominant "role"-- like the part in a drama--in order to receive those strokes and recognition for which it hungers. If the child has decided it is "not O.K." and/or others around it are "not O.K.", it will unconsciously start using ulterior transactions, that is "games", so that it can play the main role of "Victim". This is the compulsive cry-baby who sheds big tears in order to get whatever it wishes. Another role character is that of "Rescuer". Even a small child can play this role. For example, it can spend a good bit of its time and energy consoling cry-babies, although the consolation is not needed nor helpful. The drama triangle's third role of "Persecutor" is functional. Without it the other two "games" would be impossible. As the Hindi saying goes, "You need two hands to clap. With one hand alone, there is no clapping." So also, there cannot be a Victim without a Persecutor nor can there be a Rescuer without a Victim. For instance, some children in a "You're not O.K." life- position will cause constant physical and psychological pain to other children. These game-roles are played into adulthood and sometimes into ripe old age, until and unless special help and grace are given to

DAY FOUR : REMEMBERING

the "players" so that they become aware of their destructive ways of relating and choose to change.

To return to our case histories. Because as a child he was fed food that he hated by his well-meaning mother, John felt himself to be a Victim. Alex too saw himself as a Victim, who was always being "rescued" by his over-nurturing mother. She consistently directed him not only what to eat but also what quantity to take --very little, like herself.

(5) ACTING OUT THE DRAMA IN REAL LIFE: Once these early decisions, basic emotional positions, roles and life-scripts have been chosen, "the show gets on the road". The drama is lived out cautiously and haltingly at first then as adults with more consistency. The "not O.K." story is always a tragedy. This means that the hero/heroine proceeds from one failure to another until a final defeat.

In T.A. language becoming a "winner" has nothing to do with winning a prize. Nor does it mean beating out another person in competition. Living life as a "winner" means being authentic to our true selves. It means living without masks and inter- relating without pretense. In the words of Scripture being a winner happens, *"If we live by truth and in love......"* (Ep 4:15) This is not to suggest that there may not be negative episodes or lapses. Rather, it refers to our fundamental orientation of facing up humbly and gratefully to our limitations and gifts without deceit. Conversely, being a "loser" means the tragedy of consciously or unconsciously wearing masks and living a make-believe role. It means relating compulsively, most always with painful feelings--towards others, ourselves and God. The loser sees him/herself as Victim, Rescuer, or Persecutor, not knowing why or how to escape the endless round of bad feelings and painful, unsuccessful relationships.

To further exemplify, as an adult John moved into the role of Rescuer. He served Alex the amount of food he himself needed--whether Alex liked it or not. Discounting Alex's complaints, John was always smiling. Apparently a good-natured Rescuer, John often unwittingly "persecuted" others for their own good! As a child Alex took on the role of Victim. Once an adult, however, he had all the answers. Whenever in a group, he "rescued" anyone who was in need of information about anything. In this role Alex unconsciously looked down on others who were less better dressed or who knew less information than he. In other words, Alex was quietly a Persecutor. He spent his time making others feel "small". This of course was unintentional compensation for his own large inferiority complex, and his not feeling O.K.

Sharing Our Historical Burdens

Before going to share and to pray in teams, retreatants are told to choose two persons in the group, their partner and one other. Each retreatant is then asked to jot down briefly and honestly their first impressions of these two people, what sort of personalities they saw them as and their reactions to them upon first meeting. We intend using this data after the following exercises are completed.

T.A. helps us get quickly into touch with parental influences upon our personalities through use of a "life-script questionnaire". We will now use some of these life-script questions in order to awaken us to our historical roots:

(a) In writing briefly describe your mother. Say what sort of woman was she in your eyes, when you were very young, e.g. before you were big enough to go to school. It may help to close your eyes. Remember your childhood place of living and see your mother as she was typically at home with you as a child.

(b) When your mother was pleased with you, how did she show it? What did she say and do to show she was happy with you? How did you feel about it? And when she was displeased with you for whatever reason, what did she usually say or do? What did you usually feel and do in response to her behaviour of displeasure?

DAY FOUR : REMEMBERING

(c) Did she want you as her child? How did she show this? Did she ever reward you in childhood for something you had done? How did she do this? Did she ever punish you? Why and how? Describe a punishment which you remember her giving to you. What was your response to this?

Repeat this exercise for your relationship with your father. If there were any other older persons living with you when you were a small child--grandparents, aunts, uncles--do the same exercise. Read what you have written then share how you perceive these personal histories have formed you as an adult. What effect did these relationships have upon the formative elements of your personality: the kind of stroking which you received, your own early childhood decisions, your basic life-position, main role and your own chosen life-script of being "O.K." or "Not O.K.", a "winner" or "loser"?

After hearing your partners life-histories, consult your first impression of him/her. What have you learned from this? Do you agree that outward appearances are deceptive? Why?

* **COMMON REFLECTION II:** These exercises are continued during this second period also. Each sharing concludes with prayer together to express thanks and to petition healing graces. In thanking the Lord for our creation and that of our companions, we include the gift of our parents. We thank God for using limitations and negative experiences for our growth. Like beautiful *baateek* hand-prints, each of us are special, unrepeatable masterworks. Our Creating Lord never uses a person's design more than once. All human beings put together make up a fantastic panorama of beauty and variety. We thank the Holy Spirit for continuing this artistry in us and others. God is still creating us in the divine image. We express our need for healing of wounded relationships and memories.

* **HOLY HOUR :** At this stage of Day Four some retreatants go into periods of anger-resentment and sadness-depression. This is triggered by the sudden exposure to their own brokenness. Such

an experience can be shattering. This afternoon's Holy Hour should be a time of deep therapy. Christ, the Wounded Healer, brings to our personal impoverishment His infinite riches. There is consolation here by the logic of faith: the more our need, the greater His gifts (see Rm 5:17-21; 2 Co 12:7-10). All of us, particularly today during this hour, are invited to respond to His call. *"Come to me, all you who labour and are overburdened, and I will give you rest..."* (see Mt 11:28-30)

* COMMON REFLECTION III: All of us resemble our parents, physically, psychologically, and spiritually. Because they are/were impressionable pilgrims themselves, like us they too have received family likenesses from their parents. Looking at family photo albums, we smile as we recognise among members of the different generations striking similarities in stature, facial cut and colour. In an IHR we examine in depth our psychological, emotional and spiritual heritage. By God's providence, all of this forms part of the mystery which makes us who we are. We want to become aware of it, claim it all, be responsible for everything. Only by this completely honest, total acceptance can we face up to the challenges of our unfinished growth. Below is the true story of a person who was brave enough to face squarely who she was. Instead of being imprisoned by anger over her wounded past, Leela decided that she would grow where she had been transplanted by God's divine plan.

Leela, The Difficult Delhi Child

To listen to her as a young woman was to hear non-stop complaints. She criticised everything and everyone. Without knowing the reason she was a thoroughly disgruntled personality. Apparently the answer was not to be found in her parents; both were very quiet, peace-loving persons. Yet, the key to Leela's behaviour was in her family history. Here are some of its facts.

> When Leela's mother, Elizabeth, was carrying her, the whole family of five moved from a lovely Mangalorean

DAY FOUR : REMEMBERING

village home to a crowded apartment in the heart of a very hot Delhi. There Leela's father, Alfred, had to find work to support his family. Out of consideration for Elizabeth's pregnant condition, Alfred kept his financial problems to himself. A typical scene each evening was for him to come home exhausted from the day's work. Normally he had a good appetite. However, due to all the tensions and worries, he lost his taste for food. When his wife Elizabeth enquired how things were going at work, Alfred curtly answered that everything was all right and that she should not worry. But she did worry--plenty. Adapting to this new environment of a big city was unexpectedly difficult for her. She knew no Hindi or English. When she went to the bazaar each day, no one there knew Konkani, the only language she could speak. She had to be satisfied with using sign language. It was humiliating for her. At times she felt she would go out of her mind, especially when the children were at school and she was alone. Where had all the joy of life gone since the family moved to Delhi? Had she made a big mistake asking Alfred to have a fourth child? Elizabeth began to have doubts about how wise it had been to increase her family. She had not counted on all these pressures in North India. The infant inside her--who would be called Leela--picked up these disturbing vibrations. After her birth, almost as soon as she could express herself with gestures and simple words, Leela showed anger. She was clearly a disturbed, discontented child. Half jokingly Elizabeth would tell her friends that Leela was her "Delhi child". From childhood up through adolescene and adulthood Leela had recurring dreams that she was either hopelessly lost in a jungle or else she saw herself running towards some distant goal, frantically worried whether she would make it or not. But somehow before the dream ended she always did succeed in her efforts to arrive at her destination.

A TIME FOR HEALING

COMMENT: In the IHR Leela was asked by one of the animators what meaning she attached to these recurring dreams. She responded that she didn't know what they meant. Asked whether she saw any connection between her early life and her adult habit of bitter complaining, she said that she saw no relationship. Finally, there was question about a possible link between her personal problems and the fact that her family had moved from Mangalore to Delhi immediately before her birth. Again Leela had no response. So the animator asked her if she would be ready to do a Gestalt role-play. She agreed. This therapeutic technique has the person play her/him self in a critical situation of life. As though sitting on a stage, the person doing the Gestalt speaks out thoughts and feelings which she/he would have had at the time of the event which is being replayed. Opposite the person is an empty chair. At a certain point of this special psycho-drama the role-player is asked to move to the chair and speak as though she/he were the particular person who was involved with the subject doing the Gestalt in the critical incident which is being relived. The following is a summary of how this dialogue went between Leela and her phantasised mother. I do not include the animator's remarks and questions which came in between the many pauses and silences. The animator is like a director during a play-rehearsal, keeping a sharp focus on central issues of thought and feeling.

LEELA AS HERSELF (speaking in soliloquy to her Mother who is pregnant with her): Mother, you were new to Delhi. Everything was so different from Mangalore-- language, weather, customs. You weren't ready for these many changes coming all of a sudden. You were tense and anxious for Dad, too. He had to find a new job; he was also concerned about you and the adjustments you had to make. Mother, even while you were carrying me, you somehow passed on to me your own nervousness, your resentment, anger and bewilderment. I'm still carrying all these things around inside me. But I don't want to be burdened like this any longer. I've had enough of it!

DAY FOUR : REMEMBERING

LEELA AS HER MOTHER (Leela is asked to move to the empty chair opposite and respond, as though she were her mother, who has just listened to the things spoken to her above by her daughter Leela): Leela, dear, I never realised I was hurting you within my womb! I didn't have the slightest idea that I was passing on to you my own feelings of insecurity. Please, forgive me, my child! With all my love I give you the freedom you ask from all these feelings that were within me, which I somehow communicated to you, my baby.

LEELA AS HERSELF (sitting in her own chair, she is asked if she is ready unconditionally both to forgive and to ask forgiveness from her mother--and all mother-figures-- against whom she has complained throughout her life. Then she is asked if she is willing to give all this to the Lord for healing. She does it in this way): Lord, Jesus, thank you for giving me the awareness of all this. I give forgiveness to my mother. She didn't know what she was doing when she hurt me, while I was inside her. I also ask her forgiveness and that of many other people who reminded me of her. Because I see now that by my complaints I was really transferring on to her and all those others like her my anger and resentment. Lord, thank you for taking away these negative feelings through your most Precious Blood. You set me free from all this old resentment, this rebelliousness. You heal me and my memories. You heal my relationships with my mother and all these other people. Praise you Lord, Jesus!

COMMENT: When Leela came into the IHR, she was like most people-- "fragmented". She had scattered recollections of her past history. They all seemed jumbled and unconnected. Unconsciously Leela had disowned part of her self, the difficult "Delhi Child". Those memories were very painful, so she blocked them out of her awareness, she "forgot" them. This is where a Gestalt exercise helps recall memories that were thought long gone and buried in the past. Playing the roles of both herself and her mother, Leela was able to get an integrated picture of her own story. T.A. helped her understand the linkage of stroking, life position and her tragic script of being a "loser". The reconciling grace of Christ empowered her to reach out to her mother with forgiveness and sympathy. Her wounded memories were touched by the Lord because she had become aware that she was hurt deeply and needed healing. These events of the past did not change; but Leela's interpretation of them did. She came to understand herself and her mother with the mind and heart of Christ. After her Gestalt Leela felt like a new person, lightened, relieved and joyful. She exclaimed, "Oh, I didn't know I was carrying around such a weight all these years! I'm so happy and light, I feel I can fly!"

Exercises

To close this third reflection, the following exercises are suggested to the retreatants:

(1) Share with your partner/s what you know about your own birth and how you were accepted by your family. From what you know of your parents, their characteristics, is there a connection with your own personality traits, positive and negative? Explain your answer with examples from your own life.

(2) Is there any trait which has been with you most of your life of which you like to be rid? With your partner/s search out the root memory connected with the origin of this negative characteristic. The "root memory" of this event will typically be traumatic, because the event was painful. So search for a time when you were hurt. Ask yourself if you have ever forgiven the person whom you perceive to have been the cause of this suffering to you. Give the person, the event and the memory to the Lord for healing.

DAY FOUR : REMEMBERING

(3) Which negative qualities dominate your life? Which do you want to be rid of today? Using T.A. and its life-script questionnaire, see if the origin of these is not in your early family relations.

* **EUCHARISTIC CELEBRATION:** The votive Mass of the Holy Family is recommended with these readings: 1) 1 Jn 3:1-2; 4:7-16; 2) Ps 103 (the whole psalm is relevant to the theme; it may be recited as a group); 3) Lk 2:1-20. For the eucharist's penitential rite, a short litany can be composed, much like that used during Holy Saturday's Vigil Mass, but adapted to the retreat reflections. E.g. *Cantor:* "By the mystery of your conception in Mother Mary's womb," *Resp.* "Lord, heal us!" *Cantor:* "By the mystery of your nine months' gestation!" *Resp.* "Lord, heal all hurts during our own gestation!" *Cantor:* "Lord, by the mystery of your blessed birth!" *Resp.* "Lord, heal us now from any traumas during our births!"

* **NIGHT COMMON SHARING:** The animator/s are aware that some of the retreatants during prayer time may "think too much", i.e. remain only at the head level without getting into contact with their feelings. It helps at the night session to call attention to this danger of thinking too much rather than turning ourselves over completely to the Lord.

* **TEAM EVALUATION:** Here, too, a prayerful atmosphere needs be maintained so that the team listens carefully in faith to what is going on within the retreat community and what the Spirit is saying to each of the team in response. One-to-one conferences continue during all free time sessions. Gratitude by the team for the inevitable ups and downs of the retreat has a multi-valency, particularly for team spirit.

A TIME FOR HEALING

PRAYER FOR THE GRACE TO REMEMBER

(For Day Four)

Abba, Father, give me the grace to use my memory well/

To remember You with thanks, to live in Your presence with joy/

As a grateful child I bring You first my parents/

Bless them, heal them, whether they're with You or us here below/

First, I bring before You my mother/

You have sent her on mission to me/

To give me Your life and love/

Because of her own background, family scars and cares/

She could not always give me the attention I craved/

Nor the acceptance I so hungered for/

In Your holy presence, Lord, I tell her here/

"Mother, I understand, I love and forgive you"/

Lord, let me hear her say those words that cure/

"Child, my own flesh and blood, I didn't know your hurt/

Now it's mine, too, we're once again in pain of birth"/

Abba, **touch her** with Your light and my thanks/

My father **had his** own history/

His own pilgrimage before e'er I came/

You, God, entrusted me to his nurturing protection/

Due to many claims upon his attention and time/

And my own lack of words and ways to speak **my heart**/

He never knew how I longed for his closeness/

You, *Abba,* supply this for him abundantly/

My weak bond with him be strengthened/

He tells me today through You/

108

DAY FOUR : REMEMBERING

"Forgive me, child, please! God show my love for you/
It wasn't lack of fondness that I didn't show my care/
I did what I thought a father should, the best I could"/
Bless him, Father, touch him now/
Make his memories and mine be right, as You know how/
Jesus, Son, in your love of *Abba,* Spirit, Mary Joseph/
Reach and touch the wounds of tender words left unsaid/
Of expectations unfilled and hopes that died unborn/
Of hasty, nasty self-pitying memories unredeemed/
Spirit of grateful remembrances, of open sores the Balm/
Wash me clean by recollections of God's great love/
Tell my heart that Christ remembered me on Calvary/
That I've been in the Father's heart since all eternity/

_____

DAY FIVE

A TIME FOR HEALING: BY TURNING

As by your will you first strayed from God, so now turn back and search for him ten times harder; for as he has been bringing down those disasters on you, so will he rescue you and give you eternal joy.
(Ba 4:28:29)

The time is fulfilled, and the kingdom of God is close at hand. Repent, and believe the gospel. (Mk. 1:15)

* AIM OF THE DAY: (a) To continue our search for wounded root-memories in early relationships--sisters, brothers, relatives, friends; (b) to discover how authentically to repent--by *turning back from* our self-defeating games and other forms of selfishness, by *turning to* the Lord of Reality, and by *surrendering* ourselves to God in a growing, maturing personal faith-commitment.

* MORNING PRAYER: Ps 51 *("Have mercy on me, O God, in your faithful love......").* This is the famous fourth penitential psalm. It is a cry from the heart-depths of David, a person who is profoundly jolted at the faith-realisation of his own inner disorder and self-centredness (see 2 S 11-12). This penitent will not be satisfied with some mere surface changes in his life. Heart-surgery, a spiritual heart transplant, is desired. This is the biblical meaning of reprentance conversion. It has three moments or dimensions: (1) a *turning from* our selfishness, (2) a *turning to* the Lord, and (3) a *surrendering unconditionally* by obeying God's will for us forever. Radical graces are prayed for--creation of a clean heart and the gift of an entirely new, resolute spirit. The repentant David is entirely dissatisfied with the basic direction of his spiritual life. Inspired by the same Holy Spirit centuries later, Paul of Tarsus fills out the reasons why a person converting to the Lord seeks an inner transformation. Human life which is centred only upon itself is

DAY FIVE : TURNING

empty, estranged, alienated from God, closed in upon itself in the dungeon of its own limitations:

> Now that is hardly the way you have learnt Christ, unless you failed to hear him properly when you were taught what the truth is in Jesus. You were to put aside your old self, which belongs to your old way of life and is corrupted by following illusory desires. Your mind was to be renewed in spirit so that you could put on the New Man that has been created on God's principles, in the uprightness and holiness of the truth. (Ep 4:20-24)

The First Of Many Conversions

A famous psychologist has observed that the biggest problem with our modern fast-changing society is *change itself*. Change requires effort, internally and externally. This implied cost in effort, however, not everyone is ready to pay. The required adaptation is sometimes very painful and unsettling. To avoid the pain involved in all change-for-growth not a few people choose rather to become neurotically sick. Neurosis is a serious form of mental illness. Carl Jung explains that neurosis is always some form of substitution for "legitimate suffering". The neurotic tries to run away from life's unavoidable pains. Thus neurosis is like running franatically in a squirrel cage. There is no way out and the effort leads nowhere!

Christian conversion involves change and growth; it offers a paschal exodus from a meaningless, unfruitful life to an eternal, most precious glory. But it too carries a price tag. Conversion to God and participation in the divine life involves legitimate suffering, a Way of the Cross. Such passing suffering and trials, we are told by sacred scripture, are not to be compared with the prize that lies ahead of us forever. These paschal pains are like birthpangs for our promised new life in God.

> By divine power, God has lavished on us all the things we need for life and for true devotion, through the knowledge of him who has **called us by his own glory** and goodness. Through these, the greatest and price-

> *less promises have been lavished on us, that through them you should share the divine nature and escape the corruption rife in the world through disordered passion........Never allow your choice or calling to waver; then there will be no danger of your stumbling, for in this way you will be given the generous gift of entry to the eternal kingdom of our Lord and Saviour Jesus Christ.* (2 P 1:3-5,10-11)

Before Vatican II the word "conversion" was used in Catholic circles for adults who received baptism. The word also described those who changed their church affiliation. The Council, however, has gone beyond these restricted understandings. Basing itself on biblical teaching, Vatican II describes christian life as a pilgrim journey in which there is *constant need for conversion.* After talking about an adult's first conversion, the Council's *Missionary Decree* goes on to state:

> *This conversion is, indeed only initial; sufficient however to make persons realise that they have been snatched from sin, and are being led into the mystery of God's love, who invites them to establish a personal relationship with him in Christ. Under the movement of divine grace the new converts set out on a spiritual journey by means of which, while already sharing through faith in the mystery of the death and resurrection, they pass from the old man to the new man who has been made perfect in Christ (see Col 3:5-10; Ep 4:20-24). This transition, which involves a progressive change of outlook and morals, should be manifested in its social implications and effected gradually during the period of catechumenate. Since the Lord in whom they believe is a sign of contradiction (see Lk 2:34; Mt 10:34-39), the converts often have to suffer misunderstanding and separation, but they also experience those joys which are generously granted by God.* (13).

DAY FIVE : TURNING

The Church is aware she is "at once holy and always in need of purification" and that while in her pilgrim state she is called permanently to the path of repentence and renewal of faith (see *Dogmatic Constitution On The Church,* 8)

My ministry brings me into intimate contact not only with Christians, but also with Hindus, Muslims and Sikhs, people of every social level. I am struck that in so many of these pilgrims, though outwardly they differ widely, spiritually they manifest the same sense of felt-need for deepening conversion. I think this comes from the Holy Spirit of Christ who nurtures within us two profound convictions: (1) we are each called to union with an All-Holy God and because of this (2) we constantly require on-going purification. As I just said I can only attribute such a similarity of deep-seated urge towards penitential conversion to God, the Holy Spirit. This inspired thrust is discovered, like so many diamonds, not only in the Judiac-Christian traditions but also in other world religions. Take, for example, the following song which is based upon the ancient Pilgrim Hymn of the Upanishads:

> Lead me, Lord, from darkness to light/
> **From** falsehood to truth/
> **From** death to life-without-end/
> **From** fear to trust/
> **From** hatred to love/
> From violence to peace/
> May your peace, Lord, fill all hearts/
> Our families be filled with your peace/
> Our universe be filled with your peace/
> Your peace! Your peace! Your peace!

*MEDITATION: As on other mornings, entering into the Eucharistic Lord's healing presence, we want to become aware that we are *embodied* spirits. We acknowledge this by, first, deliberately putting our limbs at ease. Once the group is settled down, we prayerfully read aloud Gn 3 and reflect on this first human tragedy. It is at root of so much of our misery today including our own human mortality. During this retreat we want to become very conscious that we are not alone. Each person of this retreat group is, in a real sense, a community of people: parents, grandparents, ancestors going back centuries, not to mention present friends. We are all linked. This story of the "Fall" belongs to the human family of all generations and races. The "Second Adam and Eve"--Jesus and Mary--are exceptions to the fact that every adult who has walked across history's stage has done so not as an innocent bystander. All of us have contributed some how to the damage done to our family and to our planet. Each of us has imitated Adam and Eve, personally ratifying our solidarity in evil. Like our First Parents we also have tried to "play games" with God. We have rebelled against our Maker. We have wanted to "do our own thing" and have proudly sought to have our own way--not God's. As a special grace of this contemplation today we ask God, Spirit of holiness and conversion, to give us a deep consciousness and insight into the patterns of untruth in our lives. We ask that we realise at soul-depths the disorder and insanity of creatures wanting to be morally autonomous from an all-loving God.

* COMMON REFLECTIONS I-II: (For this morning's first session we present material for both common reflections. Its division is left to the animator's choice.) We begin with a review of the day's prayer. This daily evaluation is meant to demonstrate that obstacles to meditation are encountered by everyone. We want to identify the most common hindrances and then work out methods of overcoming them. In this way we show that we take seriously our call to be contemplatives-in-action by striving to make steady progress in prayer.

Turning From Games As A First Step To Conversion

From Day Five until the end of our IHR we shall be dealing with various dimensions of christian conversion. Today we want to reflect upon the first part of this process, the part that deals with

DAY FIVE : TURNING

turning from our systems and patterns of untruth, and *turning to* the pursuit of reality lovingly in Christ. For *turning* is at the beginning of any real conversion. It means a change of spiritual direction, a change in our thinking, in our priorities, in our motivation and finally in our behaviour.

In our desire to experience a real conversion of life, we know that we must turn from our unproductive old ways to new ways of thinking, feeling and acting "in Christ". To help us do this T.A. is a powerful human science to understand ourselves and others better, and to give us options in order to become more honest, more authentic and creative in our relationships. Before examining Genesis 3 in the light of T.A., we want first to study carefully the meaning of "Games". Eric Berne describes the "psychological game" as a recurring set of transactions between people, which are often repetitive and superficially rational but also which have a concealed motivation. In other words, as face value the game-interaction appears honest and forthright. But there is actually hidden agenda, with a hidden meaning and a surprise, painful goal in view. This goal is called the "payoff". It is the compensation, the reason why "players" consciously--more often, unconsciously--go through the gamey transaction. Its payoff is like a quick, painful kick which comes at the very end of the game. Eric Berne has put his concept of the T.A. "game" into a formula:

$$C^1 + G^2 = R^2 \dashrightarrow S^1 \dashrightarrow X^2 \dashrightarrow P^2$$

(Note: the superscripts "1" and "2" designate the first and second player in the game.)

C=*Con* of the first, or initiating, player. The *"Con"* in player one is the tendency to cheat others by using **gamey** transactions. *Con* is slang for a person convicted of or proved guilty of an offence. It may also be understood as a short form of "confidence-person", meaning someone who dishonestly wins others' confidence in order to trick them.

A TIME FOR HEALING

G= *Gimmick* in the second, or target, player. The *"Gimmick"* is a weakness or personality trait within a person whereby she/he is vulnerable to being "hooked"--like an unwary fish--into a game transaction.

R= *Response* of the second player, who has been "hooked" by the opening move of the first. The *"Response"* is like an unwary animal's moving towards a bait, not realising that there is a trap which will soon be sprung, capturing the unsuspecting animal.

S= *Switch* of the first player from a single level communication to another, surprise level transaction. In each game there is a social--overt--level communication, which is from one ego-state. Then there is a *"Switch"* to a second, hidden--convert--level of communication. This comes from another ego-state, which gives the main message of the **gamey** transaction.

X= *Double-Cross*. It is felt, like an electric shock, within the second player, who is the game's target. This *"Double-Cross"* is the split-second fluster, the mix-up and painful confusion within the second player.

P= *Payoff* in the second player, when the "kick" or shock of bad feelings gets through to the conscious level of the person victimised. The *"Payoff"* brings the game to its climax, the bitter fruit of indulging in this kind of human transaction.

Let's see how this formula works out in actual daily life. Here are two small examples.

(1)   Vanity Fair:

C[1] "Shanta, you dress better than anyone I know. Your clothes are just beautiful! I would love sometime to feast my eyes on them. Do you have a second now, for me to have just a peek at your wardrobe?

DAY FIVE : TURNING

G^2 (She is pleased and feeling flattered by her friend's compliments about her good taste. Here is a chance to show off some of her newest clothes. Shanta smiles with pleasure, not realising she is being hooked into a game.)

R^2 (Shanta replies) "Sure! I have some time. Come and see all my saries."

S^1 (The Game-player picks up a sari and holds it up to the light, examining it closely.) "Oh, this is so exquisite! My, my! Shanta, do you have any objection if I borrow it for just two days for me to wear to a wedding celebration of my cousin?"

X_2 (Shanta feels suddenly trapped and uncomfortable but she manages to say something) "Unh, Unh.......I guess I won't be using it within the next couple of days. Please do take it with you."

P^2 (Shanta now realises that she has been tricked. She feels victimised. Her sick, sour smile is in contrast with the Game-Player who beams brightly with satisfaction as she folds the sari under her arm and walks out of Shanta's home.)

(2) Tricks Of The Trade:

C^1 (Salesman in a fashionable store show a shopper some fountain pens. He speaks with great pride) "These are top-rate foreign pens!" he says. "You won't find this quality in any market around here."

G^1 (Sees them and thinks that his friends do not have such pens. They really do look special. He takes a step closer towards the sales counter.)

R^2 (He picks up one and tries writing with it on a paper pad eagerly supplied by the merchant. He asks.......) "How much is this one?"

S^1 (The sales-person nods his head approvingly) "That one is *really* high class! Professional people like it--you know, like

A TIME FOR HEALING

doctors, engineers, lawyers, successful businessmen. And since it is from out-of-country, it will be a conversation piece for you." He pauses and sighs a bit. "But then it may be a little too costly for you..."

X^2 (Reflects within himself, "Does this fellow think I'm just a common, poor nobody or what?" He feels challenged and yet doubtful because of the high cost. He wants the pen but he does not like the price. The merchant looks at him expectantly.) "I'll take it," he says with an air of decisiveness, which covers up his inner confusion.

P^2 (Paying much more money than he knows he can afford, he puts the foreign pen into his pocket. He walks away feeling surprised with himself and also a little foolish for having made this fashionable, expensive purchase.)

Retreatants are invited to relate their own typical games and analyse them. Examples from everyday life can also be used. For instance, as babies we had two kinds of crying. One was a sign to our mothers of genuine distress, which she recognised and came to our aid. The other kind of crying was for the sake of "making noise". It was a game-cry and our mothers learned to recognise it and just let us cry. Other people in the house-- like visitors--were hooked into our gamey tears. They came running to help us. Little though we were, we knew how suddenly to "switch" from crying to laughing, thus crossing up the dumbfounded rescuers and giving them a payoff of feeling stupid.

Growing older, we may have used an habitual behaviour of regularly coming late to school or handling in hometasks after the time due. All of these games were played according to formula. They were procedures which were clearly predictable. They had opening moves and endings that gave a "pay-off" of bad feelings. Why did we and others use these double-messaged transactions? Because we found them ways to pass our time. They were also proven ways of getting attention through strokes from others, positive and negative. And through these games we were unconsciously confirming

DAY FIVE : TURNING

ourselves in playing our favourite role --victim, rescuer, persecutor. T.A. offers us now a way out of these self-defeating patterns of relating with others. For, no matter what the payoff, games always result in a loss, a diminishment in both ourselves and others.

We return now to Genesis 3 and look at it in light of T.A. Before doing so, however, I wish to make clear three points. (1) I do not in any way suggest that this psychological analysis gives the whole or even the main meaning of this inspired passage. (2) I do not intend in any way to trivialise the subject's seriousness. I understand--and I want the reader to understand clearly--that more than just "bad feelings" are involved in Original Sin. At basis is human freedom in pride and false autonomy abusing its gifts and rebelling freely against God. (3) In this key scriptural text about our human origins we are dealing with not just one rebellion but a paradigm of all rebellions. In some small way T.A. can help us recognise some dimensions of this "quietly committed revolution" against the All-Good God. It bears repetition that games are habitual, compulsive and often unconscious. We try to play them with everyone, with those with whom we are closest and, yes, even with God. This is what our first parents did, as we shall now see.

The Origin Of Games As Described In Genesis

Using the text of Genesis 1-2 we have meditated upon human life as it came from an All-Loving God. As described there the first couple were transparently open to themselves, to the rest of creation and to their Creator. Adam and Eve reigned as King and Queen in beautiful harmony. This fact is incredibly important for us. Because it tells us about God's plan both for creation and recreation. Reflection upon Gn 3 tells about our "other side". Here we are introduced to the "Father of Lies", who always plays games in order to bring about our total destruction (see Jn 8:44). We have just seen how the ulterior transaction, with its hidden message and hidden motive, is of a game's essence. Notice how every statement of Satan has an insinuating message and hostile motive:

C^1 "Did God really say you were not to eat from any of the trees in the garden?"

G^2 "We may eat the fruit of the trees in the garden."

R^2 "But of the fruit of the tree in the middle of the garden God said, 'You must not eat it, nor touch it, under pain of death.'"

S^1 "No! You will not die! God knows in fact that the day you eat it your eyes will be opened and you will be like gods, knowing good from evil."

X^2 The woman saw that the fruit of the tree was good to eat and pleasing to the eye, and that it was enticing for the wisdom that it could give.

P^2 So she took some of its fruit and ate it. She also gave some to her husband who was with her, and he ate it. Then the eyes of both of them were opened and they realised that they were naked. So they sewed fig-leaves together to make themselves loin-cloths.

COMMENT: A wisdom-saying states that we can better gauge others from the quality of their questions than from their answers. Gamey people often make their first move with a question, since it is so disarming. Outwardly a question is a simple, straight-forward adult invitation in search of factual information. The "Father of Games", Satan, described by our Lord himself as a murderer from the start, begins sacred history's most treacherous transaction with a question. It is bogus. Like most calumny, its poison comes from its sublte insinuation. It misrepresents God as being unreasonable.

(Listen carefully to the question in Gn 3:1, "Did God *really* say you were not to eat from *any* of the trees in the garden?") Eve naively corrects Satan's deliberate mis-statement. In doing so she makes her first mistake: she enters into a conversation with the Tempter. In contrast to Eve the Gospel shows us the faithful, New Israel, Jesus, as He briskly rebukes the Adversary. Jesus thus conquers Satan in three generic temptations. Each one of them is repre-

DAY FIVE : TURNING

sentative of whole categories of seduction: the flesh, world, and pride of life (see Mt 4:1-11; Lk 4:1-13). In Jesus' victory over all temptations is found the way out for all those who put their trust in Him. By His example we have a partial answer to why God allows His children to be tested and tempted: that we in Christ may conquer evil as Jesus did and thus witness to God's fidelity.

> *None of the trials which have come upon you is more than a human being can stand. You can trust that God will not let you be put to the test beyond your strength, but with any trial will also provide a way out enabling you to put up with it.* (1 Co 10:13)

Eve enters into this temptation freely. To the Tempter's question she offers information. This supplies Satan with "ammunition" that will be used against Eve to overcome her. Now comes the Big Lie. The Father of Deceit brazenly accuses God of lying! Eve is now face-to-face with the fundamental temptation of all creatures: to doubt God's intentions, to see God as the real Enemy of happiness. Satan's hidden message is cleverly directed to Eve's "Free Child" ego-state: she can go right ahead and eat the forbidden fruit, despite what God says, and by so doing she will have the experience she needs to be just like a god! We know the awful shock Eve and Adam received from this carnal knowledge which they received from disobeying God. Yes, their eyes were opened, but in a very different way from what they had phantasised when relying upon Satan's promises. Still, when God confronted this first human couple with the truth, they did not acknowledge their guilt honestly. To their servile fear, guilt and shame they now add duplicity.

Yahweh: "Have you been eating from the tree I forbade you to eat?"

Adam: "It was the woman you put with me; she gave me some fruit from the tree, and I ate it."

Yahweh: "Why did you do that?"

Eve: "The snake tempted me and I ate."

Adam and Eve assume a role of the "Victim" position and deny their responsibility by trying to play a game entitled "If it weren't for this other person....." When God punishes, truthful love is expressing itself in order to heal, by inviting the sinner back to a life of living the truth in love. We see in Gn 3:16-19 that God allows us to "eat" some of the bitter fruit of our own making, the results of our own selfish choices. This is divine love withheld in order to call us back to true freedom and life. In face of this enormous human tragedy God is heard inviting these rebellious children to hope for victory over the Evil One. Addressing the snake, which symbolises Satan, God solemnly promises:

> *I shall put enimity between you and the woman, and between your offspring and hers; it will bruise your head and you will strike its heel.* (Gn 3:15)

This verse is called the *proto-evangelium*–the original goodnews. The church interprets this ancient verse as referring to Christ's future victory over all evil. The woman of the text is prophetic of Mary's role as the new Eve, mother of the Redeemer.

From Parents To Children: The Vicious Games Continue

In Genesis 4 we see how the human spirit becomes rebellious even against its own flesh and blood. Cain was a farmer, his brother Abel a shepherd. One day the two offered sacrifice to God and Abel's found divine favour. Filled with jealousy Cain became downcast. God then warned him:

> *If you are doing right, surely you ought to hold your head high! But if you are not doing right, Sin is crouching at the door hungry to get you. You can still master him.* (Gn. 4:7)

Instead of heeding this caution, like his mother Eve, Cain decides to do things his own way--not God's way. Treacherously, under guise of fraternal intimacy--going for a walk together-- Cain murders

DAY FIVE : TURNING

his younger brother. After his sin the very same pattern of gamey denial is used by Cain as was used by his parents after theirs. God is portrayed in Gn 4:9 seeking out the criminal Cain and confronts him with his homicide:

Yahweh: "Where is your brother Abel?"

Cain: "I do not know. Am I my brother's guardian?"

Yahweh: "Listen! Your brother's blood is crying out to me from the ground. Now be cursed and banned from the ground that has opened its mouth to receive your brother's blood at your hands."

With infinite goodness and love, God gives a corrective punishment to Cain by allowing him to experience a small part of his sin's ugly disorder. In this way God calls him to turn from his brutal self-centredness and return to the path of loving relationship with others. Despite God's insistent invitations, untruth and murder multiplied. Within a few lines, the author of this early family history depicts one of Cain's descendants, Lamech, barbaricly boasting in song of his ferocity towards enemies:

Adah and Zillah, hear my voice/

wives of Lamech, listen to what I say/

I killed a man for wounding me/

a boy for striking me/

Sevenfold vengeance for Cain/

but seventy-sevenfold for Lamech/ (Gn 4:23-24)

The Chain Reaction Pattern Of Games

In every IIR one of the big discovery areas is that of feelings. Retreatants come to realise not only that they have their own feelings but that those feelings have been many times hurt by other people. Because of wounded feelings and the wounded memories that go with them, a "chain reaction" of hostility is established. One hurt sets up the person for another. An example from everyday life:

One day a sister of mine asked me, "What's wrong? You look like you're searching for something." "Yes," I answered, "I've misplaced my wristwatch. I've got an important appointment and I don't want to be late. What time is it?" My sister answered, "How stupid are you? You can't even keep track of your own watch?" Ouch! That remark hurt my pride. I felt angry and victimised. All I did was ask the time. What sort of answer do I get in return? After a few minutes I started feeling ashamed of myself. "I deserved the rebuff," I thought. "I am forgetful and careless about where I put my belongings." Without realising it, I was testy and angry for most of that morning. After lunch someone asked me a simple question, and I blasted her for interrupting my work. I regretted the remark almost as soon as I made it. Here I am, the Big Martyr, now doing the very thing which I criticised others for doing.

To give another example. We have heard about the office employee who was scolded by his manager for not doing his accounts properly. When this man went home in the evening, he shouted at his wife for not preparing the kind of food he wanted. A little later the wife verbally abused her daughter for not keeping her room tidy. Finally, the daughter slapped her pet dog for being so lazy!

Wounded Family Relationships

The games we have learned to play in early childhood within our family circle we continue to play later in adulthood--until and unless we are called to awareness by professional help and/or God's grace of conversion. In Day Four of the retreat we examined our hurt memories in relationships with parents. Today we want to examine wounded root memories of relationships with close relatives: maternal/paternal grandparents, aunts/uncles, sisters/brothers, cousins, and friends. To help start reflection in this area of healing, I present now the history of Jill. This account is of real people; only names have been changed to protect privacy.

DAY FIVE : TURNING

As very small children Jack and Jill appeared to be happy brother and sister. As they grew, however, Jill noticed what she considered favouritism in the way her parents dealt with Jack and her. Because she was a girl, she said, she couldn't do many things Jack was allowed and encouraged to do by the family. Jill thought her brother was pampered. Gradually she developed a jealousy towards him and began finding fault with everything he did. She put Jack down on every occasion. After her schooling Jill became a professional stenographer. When she came to her first IHR, Jill described what she called some strong negative tensions with the male staff in her place of work. She claimed that there was much inequality in the way her company treated its male and female employees. Women always seemed to be dealt with as second class people. Whenever Jill talked about this injustice, she was surprised that she showed so much anger and resentment. Her teary outbursts caused further tension in the office. She didn't understand why all this had to happen to her. In the retreat she talked about this situation as "my cross".

COMMENT: Jill was absolutely blank on whether there was any causal connection between her early brother relationship with Jack and her present tensions with male staff workers. She was unaware that her brother relationship was being projected onto the men in her office. The internal integration of her experiences began to take shape when the IHR animator asked her about what dreams she had recently. She answered:

> Again and again I have a frightening dream of some man, like a thief, who comes near me and snatches away everything I have . . I also often dream that I am fighting with a wild elephant.

Dream analysis has been called the royal road--or way--to Integration of personality. This is demonstrated in Jill's inner healing. What had been hidden in her unconscious for years often bubbled up into her consciousness through the medium of dreams. Once she described these recurring themes in her nightmares, she was ready for a real breakthrough in awareness. It finally came by an insightful exchange between Jill and the retreat animator. Here is a summary of how that realisation came about:

Animator: "Jill, at home is there anyone who seems to be always wanting to snatch away your things--like that thief in your dreams?"

Jill: "My brother, Jack!"

Animator: "How would you briefly describe your behaviour with your brother?"

Jill: "I am constantly fighting with him."

Animator: "Is your situation something like that struggle you see in your dreams with the elephant?"

Jill: (she nods)

Animator: "And how do you feel towards Jack?

Jill: "I feel very angry."

Animator: "Jill, what can you do now about this situation, as a responsible adult woman?"

Jill: "I can talk to Jack and to my parents about my needs......I can also buy whatever I need for myself; I have my own money....... I really don't have to depend upon others the way I have."

This exchange brought deep understanding to Jill about the root cause of her office tensions. It also brought to the surface the wounded root memories from early childhood, when Jill first began to feel anger and jealousy towards Jack. Her parents seemed to prefer her brother to herself because Jack was a boy and she a girl. Jill had no difficulty doing a successful Gestalt with her parents, with Jack, and with the male members of her office staff. She went through a short, prayerful ritual in the Lord's healing presence of giving and receiving unconditional forgiveness with each of these people. She exchanged Christ's peace and love with them. Finally, she gave thanks to the Lord for transforming her hurt recollections from jealousy and anger to forgiveness and joy. Her own prayer to the Lord was particularly touching:

DAY FIVE : TURNING

"Lord, Jesus, whenever I needed things in the past, I could have let You know! But I didn't. I could have let my parents and Jack know, too. Instead of doing this, I kept my jealousy and anger and bitterness within myself. I suffered a lot of unnecessary pain. And I made others suffer also--Jack, my parents, the men in my office. Thank You, Lord, for healing me and my relationship with all these other people!"

Sharing In Teams

As usual, the first and second common sessions are concluded by retreatants sharing in teams. Suggested topics for this are:-

(1) OUR FAVOURITE GAMES AND HURT FEELINGS. Negative ("bad") feelings we experienced from early childhood are often the "payoff", or end-product, of games. Unaware, in our memories we can collect these hurt feelings, as though we were collecting stamps, until we have the big trade-off in the form of sickness, suicide and even murder. These feelings can be classified according to the game position we were playing when we collected them. There are feelings typical of the "Victim", "Rescuer" and "Persecutor". These three game positions of the Drama Triangle also give us a clear insight into the kinds of game transactions we have played or are still playing. We now share with our partner/s our discoveries of what kind of games and feelings we have experienced, especially in relationships with close relatives, friends, neighbours. After sharing we then pray with each other for inner healing. (2) OUR CHILDHOOD PROJECTIONS. Tell your partner/s how you have projected on to others in your adult life your early childhood gamey behaviour. Conclude by giving with the Lord Jesus unconditional forgiveness to those who hurt us. We also ask forgiveness in our hearts from those we have hurt. Likewise we exchange unconditional love and thanksgiving with these significant people in our lives. (3) OUR TURNING FROM AND TURNING TO. Christ, the Liberator-Healer, calls us out of our old patterns of thinking, feeling and misjudging to a conversion and transformation of life in Him.

A TIME FOR HEALING

> *When I was a child, I used to talk like a child, and see things as a child does, and think like a child; but now that I have become an adult, I have finished with all childish ways.* (1 Co 13:11-12)

This summons to leave our games behind and to grow up in Christ's ways comes to us today. Share with your partner/s from which games you have decided to turn. In place of these dysfunctional ways of relating, what have you decided to turn to, to follow? Pray for each other, asking the gift of power from Christ's Holy Spirit to strengthen your inner resolve.

* HOLY HOUR : The Lord Jesus through his Holy Spirit is the most active human being in creation. He is present now in the Eucharist to heal and to save. He just does not "sit there" on the altar. He continues his mission of making us whole and strong. Do we believe this? Do we affirm that the Person who spoke the following sentence is now present to save us also?

> *This text is being fulfilled today even while you are listening.* (Lk 4:21-22)

The bondage and oppression described by Jesus in Lk 4:18 applies to games as well. We are invited today to let go of our games and let God empower us to live the truth in love. This is authentic conversion.

* COMMON REFLECTION III: After a short review of how our prayer went during the Holy Hour, we move on to an essential component of every IHR, renewal and development of God's gift to us in baptism and faith. To do this it is important, at the outset, to keep in mind the three different meanings of "faith". First, the word faith may refer to the CONTENT OF OUR BELIEF. In this sense we speak of the Apostles' Creed as being a summary of christian faith. Secondly, faith may be used to mean the GIFT OF GOD by which we believe. Thus Jesus tells us solemnly:

DAY FIVE : TURNING

> *No one can come to me unless drawn by the Father who sent me .. This is why I told you that no one could come to me except by the gift of the Father.* (Jn 6:44,65)

Third, the sense in which we shall be using it now, *faith* designates OUR RESPONSE to God's divine revelation. Revelation is the most personalistic act, both divine and human. Divine revelation involves God's own self-gift offered to us in Jesus, our Way to the Father. If we commit ourselves in faith and continue till the end of our pilgrim lives to respond to this divine gift generously, God's Spirit brings our human-divine lives to a plentitude of beauty, goodness and holiness.

> *"Indeed, from his fullness we have, all of us, received-- one gift replacing another" (Jn 1:16). "My dear friends we are already God's children, but what we shall be in the future has not yet been revealed. We are well aware that when he appears we shall be like him, because we shall see him as he really is."* (1 Jn 3:2)

It is essentially important to realise that our lives are a RESPONSE TO GOD'S OWN SELF-GIFT. St. John insists that it is not we who loved God first but God who loved us and sent Jesus, God's only Son, to expiate our sins. The purpose of Christ's Coming is that we may believe personally in Him and by so doing live in communion with God and all God's children with justice and truth. In this way we are enabled always to abide in God's love. We thus share in God's Spirit, so that divine love may come to perfection in us (see 1 Jn 4:7-21). Vatican II states that God's will is that all people should have access to the Father, through Christ, the Word made flesh, in the Holy Spirit. In this way we "become sharers in the divine nature". The invisible God from the fullness of divine love addresses us as friends. In the person of Jesus God moves among us, in order to invite and receive us into His own company (see *Dogmatic Constitution On Divine Revelation,* 2).

The New Testament abounds in different figures and ways of expressing this call to respond in personal, living faith. One of the most picturesque and telling parables is that of the sower (Mk 4:1-20). In an IHR with the Spirit's necessary help we attempt to clear away the weeds and thorns that choke to death the faith which has been sown lovingly in our hearts by God's Word. Better to appreciate our responsibility to grow and mature in precious gift so that we yield 30, 60 and a 100 fold, it helps to understand the process of faith-maturation. We see this in the various levels of faith-growth. Here is a short outline to indicate the main steps in our pilgrimage to grow into the promised plentitude of Christ's life through faith-unto-fullness.

(Note: It is necessary to state that the names used below to describe the stages of faith are not normative or chronological. They are descriptive of a process; and they may be applied to individuals, families and even whole communities (parish/diocese). See, for example, St. Paul's descriptions of the faith in the early churches at Corinth, Ephesus, Thessolonica and Rome.

I   PRE-PERSONALISED STAGES:
1) Infantile (Symbiotic) Faith
2) Imitative (Cultural) Faith

II   PERSONALISED STAGES: (Note: a paschal experience of deepening conversion precedes each of these stages)
3) Personal (Covenantal) Faith
4) Community-Building (Ecclesial) Faith
5) Kingdom-Building (Apostolic) Faith
6) Cosmic (Universal) Faith

A word on each of these stages.

(1) INFANTILE FAITH: It is a stage of faith that may also be called *symbiotic* (literally, two-lives-in-one). This descriptive term suggests an analogy of mother and child during the gestation period. The infant cannot live by itself, but only in total reliance upon its mother. So too is there a complete dependency for life-support of

the believer/s upon the person who channels faith to them--e.g. an evangelist, pastor, or parent. Like a mother physically nurturing her child, it is very clear from his letters St. Paul understood that the young church-communities which he had founded could not survive without regular faith- support supplied to them by himself and other pastors. In its earliest stage, faith is symbiotic. Its strength is awfully vulnerable and fragile. Constant pastoral visiting, exhortation, teaching, witness and sacramental ministering are essential for it to survive. In this sense, especially for young children and many adult catechumens, faith is not so much "taught" as "caught".

(2) IMITATIVE FAITH: All human learning comes about by some form of comparison and imitation. A small child learns by imitating. Lying on its back an infant learns to smile by mirroring its mother. Around the eleventh month it imitates elders in taking its first steps. And so for most other skills the baby will learn throughout life, it will be copying what is seen from others. This is also true for faith's second growth stage. The child learns to fold its hands in prayer, to sign itself with the cross, to kiss sacred objects, and to behave properly during the eucharist by watching the elders. Hence, clear, consistent good example is needed from parents and other members of the family in order to foster right religious attitudes, values and behaviour in children. For this reason, Vatican II calls christian families the "domestic church". Without its witness, children's faith will not mature properly. On the other hand, this stage of faith-maturation is also referred to as *"cultural christianity"*. The devotee, young or old, goes through all the outward motions of the faithful, without having as yet personalised the culturally inherited faith or committed oneself to Christ. Faith-life at this second level is other-directed; it is controlled in a way by the community's expectations and customs. This is perfectly acceptable and inevitable for young children. It is a healthy stage of development. But in adolescents and adults, if their faith is fixated at this level, it means they have the outward forms but no inner convictions. They "follow the leader", complying with external cultural and religious traditions without understanding or personal commitment. This quality of religion can easily turn into empty ritual or even superstition and

magic. In Acts 8:9-24 Peter is shown confronting Simon, who was a magical christian. So fascinated by the charismatic phenomenon accompanying Philip's ministry among the Samaritans, Simon was ready to pay any amount of money in order to make this mysterious gift his own. He obviously had phantasies of gaining large economic profits by putting these holy powers of the Spirit to commercial use. (From this incident we get the word "simony", which refers to the sin of Simon, the man who wanted to buy/sell the sacred.)

(3) PERSONAL FAITH: This is also called *covenantal* faith. At this level the devotee as a responsible person freely accepts Christ's invitation of mutual self-gift. Thereby she/he enters into a covenant relation with God through Christ in the Spirit forever. If the believer were a non-christian, the next steps after making this act of saving faith would be entrance into a catechumenate and --after some period of formation--celebration of total commitment by reception of the sacraments of christian initiation: baptism, confirmation and eucharist. For those who have already been sacramentalised, to arrive at a personal faith *they must be evangelised* (see Rm 10:14-15). This can and does happen during retreats. An evangelist must present the Good News to them in such a way that they realise for the first time in their lives that Jesus Christ, the living Lord, is inviting them into personal communion with God for life eternal. The evangelised are helped to realise that God is offering divine life to them as personal Self-Gift; nothing less than total self- gift in return suffices. Hence all the elements of an authentic conversion are needed: (1) freely turning from a selfish life; (2) turning in love to Christ, the living Lord; and (3) unconditionally surrendering oneself to Christ forever. This is the "obedience of faith" to God's Word (see Rm 1:6). It is a saving act because it involves the whole person in an act of sacrifice--of mind, heart soul, and all relationships--to God (see Dt 6:4-5: Mt 22:37-40).

(4) COMMUNITY-BUILDING FAITH: This next stage of repentance- conversion expands the faith vision and commitment so as actively include the whole community of believers. For this reason it can also be called *ecclesial* faith. We can see this kind of faith in

the post-resurrection gospel accounts and also in the opening chapter of Acts. Converted personally to Christ by the Good Friday-Easter Sunday experience the disciples are gathered by the Spirit into a close-knit community. *"With one heart all these joined constantly in prayer, together with some women, including Mary the mother of Jesus, and with his brothers"* (Ac 1:14). This ecclesial level of faith is not arrived at without another conversion of mind and heart. When it takes place, the believer for the first time in personalised faith can pray, "I believe in the holy, catholic Church." The breadth of faith is broadened from the person of Jesus Christ to include his family, his Body. A good analogy can be seen in married life. When two young people celebrate the covenant of marriage, this implies that their love is open to their spouse's family. However, this readiness to enter into relationship with the other's relatives is actualised only gradually. Indeed there must be a kind of on-going conversion so that the marriage partner also "espouses" the loved one's own kith and kin, warts and all! If this does not happen, the marriage relationship of the spouses is somehow impoverished. In the same way, embracing Christ in the covenant bond of baptism implies embracing his whole family, the Church. If this does not take place, faith is prevented from developing. It can easily become individualistic, immature and sterile. It would be a huge distortion of personal faith were someone to state that she/he loves Christ but wants nothing to do with his Church! Throughout Acts and the apostolic letters we read the most beautiful and powerful descriptions of Community-Building Faith, inspired by Christ's Holy Spirit. It is only by fidelity to the Spirit that a convinced Christian's faith grows in breadth through being an active, participating member of Christ's Body. The conversion, then, is turning from individualistic attitudes to becoming truly *communitarian*-- without being exclusive or communalistic towards members of other religions.

(5) **KINGDOM-BUILDING FAITH:** St. Luke's account of the glorified life of Jesus is very educative. There is a continuity of his gospel story and its sequel, the *Acts of the Apostles*. Before Pentecost the small band of Jewish Christians are shown as faithful to Jesus and to ecclesial fellowship, but at that stage the Church's

faith is not apostolic. The believers are not ready to implement the Kingdom's vision, *"Go out to the whole world; proclaim the gospel to all creation......'* (Mk 16:15-16); *"Go, therefore, make disciples of all nations......"* (Mk 28:19). In one of John's post-resurrection narratives he gives the detail that *"the doors were closed in the room where the disciples were, for fear of the Jews."* (Jn 20:19). God's Holy Spirit was needed to help the first Christians mature in faith. A conversion was needed in mind and heart. Luke's narrative of what happened at the first Pentecost (Ac 2:1-41), the event and also its results, portrays an expansive faith-community which embraces the whole human race as part of Christ's Kingdom for hastening the Reign of God. This is another conversion. Disciples become apostles. The community becomes apostolic only under inspiration of the Spirit and in constant obedience to the Spirit's guidance. Kingdom-Building Faith means transcending the narrow concerns of an institution and indeed of all cultural boundaries in order to embrace the whole human family. We see this happening at the Council of Jerusalem (see Ac 15:5-29). Vatican II is another milestone in Church History, in which Kingdom-Building Faith is clearly expressed. Such a faith needs be witnessed to by Indian Christians today where they are a tiny minority. So many of our non-Christian sisters and brothers are suffering under grave injustices. They are deprived of the minimum amount of help in order to grow and to develop as human persons. Working for integral development of all peoples in India is an urgent requirement of a mature christian faith. In his encyclical letter entitled *"Mission Of The Redeemer"* John Paul II explains the close link between evangelisation and integral development:

> *Through the gospel message, the Church offers a force for liberation which development precisely because it leads to conversion of heart and of ways of thinking, fosters the recognition of each person's dignity, encourages solidarity, commitment and service of one's neighbour, and gives everyone a place in God's plan, which is the building of his kingdom of peace and justice, beginning already in this life. This is the biblical perspective of the "new heavens and a new earth",*

DAY FIVE : TURNING

which has been the stimulus and goal for humankind's advancement in history. People's development derives from God, and from the model of Jesus--God and man--and must lead back to God. That is why there is a close connection between the proclamation of the Gospel and human promotion (59).

(6) **COSMIC FAITH:** This final stage of development is also called *universal* faith, because it includes the whole of creation, seen as gifts of God and part of Christian stewardship in the care of our planet. We see this in St. Paul's letters and in the lives of the saints and mystics--like Francis of Assisi, Thomas of Aquinas, Catherine of Siena, Ignatius of Loyola, Therese of Lisieux, and John XXIII. This faith gives the believer an inclusive vision of the whole of the cosmos, of all creation, as coming from God and tending back to God for its fulfillment. As for all other personalised faith levels, cosmic faith demands a deep conversion of reverence and service towards all creatures as divine gifts through the Son, in whom all things are made. Authentic ecology today needs such universal faith and its implications for protection of our endangered planet. Read psalm 148, which is a cosmic hymn of praise. It is recited by pious Jewish faithful every morning.

* **EUCHARISTIC CELEBRATION:** In keeping with the theme of conversion, of turning from/turning to, a Mass for deceased family members is recommended in order to foster a faith-sense of solidarity with the communion of saints, the Pilgrim Church with the Church in Purification and in Glory. The Third Eucharistic Prayer for young people may be used. At the commemoration of the dead there should be a slightly extended silence to allow each of the retreatants to recall their deceased relatives. For the readings: 1) 2 M 12:38-45 or 1 Th 4:13-18 or Ba 4:21-20; 2) Ps 51:6-15; 3) Jn 11:17-44.

* **NIGHT COMMON SHARING:** At the beginning of each of these sharing sessions the animator does well to summarise its purpose: a) to foster the group's faith through individual witnessing, b) to

A TIME FOR HEALING

give God our Father the glory for graces received during the day, c) to give as many people as possible a chance to share their day's pilgrim journey briefly and to the point. It may be that there is only darkness, struggle and pain to report. This too can and will build up the community through prayer and mutual concern for each other's progress.

*** TEAM EVALUATION:** One of the temptations for staff members in an IHR is to be so taken up in counselling as to neglect one's own rest and individual prayer life. To keep a balance between appropriate self-care and pastoral care is at times not an easy thing to do, especially if IHR is a regular ministry. These retreats can be exhausting and therefore draining, both physically and spiritually. Adequate rest and relaxation, then, is an issue that needs to be faced during team evaluation time.

PRAYER FOR THE GRACE TO TURN

(For Day Five)

Abba, Father, from the day of my infant cleansing/
Your burning flame has been within/
Directing this pilgrim child on a pilgrim planet/
Correcting my course from wayward paths towards You/

Jesus, Light to find the high road at night/
Midst the darkness and confusion, fear and death/
Resurrection promise, unseen Lord, my Hope/
Help my less than mustard-seed-faith to grow, to blossom
    in Thee/

Spirit, work your wonders once again/
In the upper room of this retreat community/
Grace me with my friends to turn from petty, private occupations/
Stretch my heart to love your world, send me forth for God's
    glory/

DAY SIX

A TIME FOR HEALING: BY FORGIVING

> Yes, if you forgive others their failings, your heavenly Father will forgive you yours; but if you do not forgive others, your Father will not forgive your failings either. (Mt 6:14-15)

* AIM OF THE DAY: (a) to go more deeply into the conversion process by forgiving unconditionally those who have hurt us; (b) to examine the issues of resentment and rejection that are so common but which block authentic repentance and growth in faith, hope and love.

* MORNING PRAYER: Psalm 41 *("Blessed is anyone who cares for the poor and the weak......").* This is a song of David, who has been the victim of treachery by a close companion. The gospel uses verse 9 of this psalm to describe Judas' betrayal of Jesus (see Jn 13:18), *"Even my trusted friend on whom I relied, who shared my table, takes advantage of me."* By praying psalm 41 we wish to focus especially on Jesus, who was the most rejected of human beings. How did He respond? Today the retreatants are encouraged to study this part of Jesus' personality not only in relationship with the apostle Judas (see Jn 13:21-30) but also with Peter (see Lk 22:31-34; Mt 26:31-35; Mk 14:27-31; Jn 13:36-38), and with ourselves, who so often have been guilty of big and little daily treacheries. The affective side of Jesus, his feelings and emotions, are not unimportant. In this retreat we are discovering our own feelings at a deeper level. This awareness can be unsettling. We need a model, someone who *"is not incapable of feeling our weaknesses with us, but has been put to the test in exactly the same way as ourselves, apart from sin."* (Heb 4:15-16). Jesus too like us felt resentment, rejection, anger and outrage. So we need have no fear in approaching Him, the living Lord, the Wounded Healer, to receive mercy and healing, to find grace when we need it.

*MEDITATION: We suggest meditation upon Jesus rejected by his own friends and relatives. This was not just in his passion and death. Jesus met with misunderstanding and rejection throughout his life, starting at his birth, with the slaughter of the Innocents by King Herod. The animator may suggest a number of scenes, leaving the choice to each retreatant. E.g. Mk 3:20-21; 6:1-6; Lk 4:23-30; Jn 6:59-66; 6:67-71.

* COMMON REFLECTION I-III: These three sessions leave relatively more time to personal sharing and praying for reconciliation in teams. Presentations during today's common reflections include the three dimensions of forgiveness: (1) a strong biblical basis for christian pardon; (2) psychological insights into healthy ways to deal with issues of anger, rejection, resentment, rage; and (3) some first-person case studies. The mixture of these elements is left to the animator's choice.

The Biblical Teaching On Pardon

For the first five days of our retreat we have been reflecting on the need of awareness, acceptance and forgiveness. In Day Six we want to discover that the moral demand for christian pardon is solidly based in divine revelation's insistence that mercy is God's greatest work. As for the parent, so for the children: *"Be compassionate just as your Father is compassionate"* (Lk 6:36). We can never hear enough that morality is founded upon the dogmatic certitude of God's own goodness. Moral rectitude is imitation of God. Biblically, pardon is not due to anyone; it is a gift of God. Sin incurs a debt and God, whose ways are not ours, forgives us sinners graciously. God, then, is the model for pardon. God's mercy and pardon are recurring themes throughout the bible. We have already seen that the *proto-evangelium* promises a saviour to humanity's first sinner's (see Gn 3;15). The story of Joseph (Genesis chapters 37-50) is a wonderful lesson of family pardon and restoration. Moses and David are described as long-suffering and merciful. These are preparations for the Man of Mercy, Jesus, who brings divine revelation of God's forgiving love to its highest peak. Jesus grounds his moral teaching of pardon in God's own

DAY SIX: FORGIVING

nature. "You must therefore set no bounds to your love, just as your heavenly Father sets none to his" (Mt 5:48). "Yes, if you forgive others their failings, your heavenly Father will forgive you yours; but if you do not forgive others, your Father will not forgive your failings either" (Mt 6:14-15). This explains Jesus' insistence upon a reconciled heart *before* offering prayer to the Father:

> *So, then, if you are bringing your offering to the altar and there remember that your brother has something against you, leave your offering there, before the altar, go and be reconciled with your brother first, and then come back and present your offering. (Mt. 5:23-24)*

> *And when you stand in prayer, forgive whatever you have against anybody, so that your Father in heaven may forgive your failings too.* (Mk 11:25)

One of the sternest teachings of Jesus is found in the parable of the unforgiving debtor (Mt 18:23-35). Jesus' most tender description of the Father's merciful love is the triple set of parables of lost sheep, lost money and lost son (Lk 15:1-32), in which God's paternal/maternal love, as compared with human standards, is shown to be most prodigal in giving and forgiving. The apostle John warns that if anyone is well off in worldly possessions and sees his brother in need but closes his heart to him, the love of God cannot be in him (see 1 Jn 3:17). Such a person has closed his heart to one of God's children in distress, and this means closing ourselves to God. Whether it be giving things (Mt 25:31-46) or giving pardon (Mt 18:21-22), the norm is a "seventy-seven times"--meaning God's unlimited measure of sharing. St. Paul climaxes his depiction of a morally abandoned and utterly degraded society as a people without pity (see Rm 1:24-32). In his exhortations to early christian communities the Apostle always returns to the example of God:

> *Be generous to one another, sympathetic, forgiving each other as readily as God forgave you in Christ.* (Ep 4:32)

The biblical lesson, then, is unambiguously clear: if we desire to live with God in communion of peace in this life and in life eternal we must obey the Holy Spirit within us who prompts us to imitate the Father in a giving/forgiving love according to divine generosity.

Some Helpful Hints From Human Sciences

Within the past several decades there has been a growing amount of reflection and publications about the need to take seriously that anger, resentment and rage which exists in our country's oppressed peoples. India's outcastes, her depressed castes, aboriginal and other minority communities number hundreds of millions of human beings who have been in the past and continue today to be outraged socially, politically, economically and religiously. In families of every class of Indians there are spouses and children of alcoholic and drug dependants who have suffered deep wounds from physical and moral abuse every day. In other words, there is a massive amount of oppression and pain in contemporary Indian society. We bring these hurts and oppresions into our retreat. The question is how are we to deal with this mountain of human misery?

Some practical lessons we learn from human sciences will help us in IHRs to deal with these issues realistically: (1) Do not hurry the process of healing and reconciliation by superificial, careless recourse to "quick-fix" formulas, whether psychological or religious. The way of healing may very well be a life-long struggle of recovery. Relief and power to live with the pain lie in experiencing the conviction that are on the right road with the Lord and his people. (2) On the other hand, do not hold on to anger and rage too long. One thing is to become aware of it and accept it as mine/ours, another thing is to nurture rage to the point of self-pity, suicide or homicide. (3) Each individual will have her/his own pace of inner healing; because each person's condition of pilgrimage is unique.

First-Person Histories Of Forgiveness

(1) John's struggle for justice from his brother:

We were a family of three boys. Being the eldest, I looked after my younger brothers when they were

DAY SIX: FORGIVING

children. I helped them with money so they could get a good schooling. Out of my own pocket I got each of them some property close to my house. I helped them settle their marriages and build their homes. After receiving all this from me, my brothers turned their faces against me. They even told me not to pass through their compounds. Whenever I came close to them, they threw abuses at me. After suffering this kind of treatment from them, I finally decided not to have anything to do with them. So I simply ignored them. This went on for quite a while. Then one of my brothers came to me asking money for his daughter's marriage. When I told him I had no money, he suggested that I take a bank loan by mortgaging my property. I saw his great need so I gave him my land ownership papers for him to get a bank loan. That was twelve years ago. I still haven't received my land papers back. His daughter did not get married for a long time, and I know he did not use that mortgage money for her marriage. Often I have thought, "How unjust this is!" I have carried around with me a heavy feeling of resentment for years. During this retreat I decided to forgive my brother. I did. Now experience that the Lord has really healed me, even of the feelings of anger and resentment towards him and my other brother.

COMMENT: A key to John's decision to be reconciled with his brothers revolves around the correction of his concept of justice. He is a just person himself and he expects justice from everyone. John's position before the IHR was this: *until and unless* his brothers repented of their unjust behaviour towards him, he would not forgive them. In other words John was allowing his brothers' continuing injustice to be a determinant in his withholding forgiveness. When he heard about Christ's unconditional love on the cross for him, he learned that he too must love and forgive like Christ. For, God loved us *while we were still sinners* (see Rm 5;10). In other words, John discovered that he did not have to wait for his brothers' conversions before he himself could be healed. As God had unconditionally forgiven him, so he decided that he must forgive his brothers even though they were still being dishonest and unjust

A TIME FOR HEALING

towards him. The second thing to be noted is that John's giving forgiveness does not rule out the possibility that he may have to protect himself and his own family by resorting to law if necessary. A third dimension to this healing is the following important reality. The reconciliation which John experienced during the IHR is not the end of his struggle. While it is a major step in his healing, there is still recovery work he has to do. Like successful surgery for cancer, there is aftercare needed to see that the wound does not get infected. So too for John. He knows that in Christ's healing touch is his own healing. He also realises that he must keep offering thanks and petition for a complete transformation of this relationship with his brothers, especially for healing of his wounded feelings. This will require him to keep his brothers "soaked" in the love of Christ through repeated mediatory prayer.

(2) Life as daughter of an alcoholic, Tara's story:

> We were four children in the family, two boys and two girls. I was the youngest. Today there are only two of us left. The third child, my sister, died when I was still very small and my elder brother passed away when I was an aspirant in a religious congregation. Throughout early childhood my family was very poor. Daddy used to drink liquor very much and there was no peace at home. I used to hate my father when he was drunk. In fact one day when he had come home in a drunken state and fell asleep, I beat him with a stick. Later I was to feel very ashamed and guilty because of this action of mine. Since I was the only girl my mother did not want me to be educated. She used to call me "a female dog!" I remember another time, when I was in ninth class, I was very thin and fragile, but I took studies as seriously as I could. Mother said that I did not eat food but books. At school the boys abused me by calling me nicknames that ridiculed me. At home I received constant scoldings and sometimes I really feared that I would be killed by my own family. As a religious candidate I was treated badly and twice I was told to leave the congregation

DAY SIX : FORGIVING

because it was not ready to accept me. In postulancy again I was warned that I was not fit for religious life. During a home visit my family brought in a *Pujaree* to perform magic spells over me. Even as a religious sister I often get insults spoken to me to my face. For years I wanted to be a singer, but whenever I tried out for the choir my throat became blocked and I simply could not sing. When others sang, I felt sad and also angry.

COMMENT: When Tara was asked about her deceased sister, she said she could not remember anything. However, during the course of the retreat she discovered that, young though she was, Tara actually grieved deeply for her dead sister. In childhood she had "swallowed" this grief. Rather than expressing and working through it, Tara had kept it inside her for many years. Not until her first IHR, when she was an adult woman and a religious sister, did Tara express her childhood grief, sadness and anger for the death of her sister. Early in life Tara saw herself as a "Victim". She expected to find a "Persecutor" wherever she went, and she was never long disappointed! Sometimes in her suppressed anger Tara moved quickly over to a Persecutor's position. This, of course, surprised her--as for example, when she physically attacked her father in his drunken sleep. The retreat brought about a breakthrough in Tara's awareness and helped her accept the fact that she had never fully grieved for her dead sister. She had kept all the grief inside. She also was able to accept the fact that she had unconsciously been playing "games" in her relationships. These she saw were not helping her or her interpersonal relationships. She rejected them in favour of being responsible and of pursuing reality whatever the cost. Tara mentions another significant fact. She confesses both to her longterm desire to sing and her apparent physical inability to do so. When inner healing comes to a person like Tara, she relaxes spiritually, psychologically and physically. I will not be surprised to hear from her that she is now singing beautifully for the Lord. His healing graces during the retreat set her free from grief and anger. What has happened to others can certainly happen to Tara, that her interior liberation also frees her vocal chords to praise his goodness. Being the daughter

A TIME FOR HEALING

of a serious alcoholic, her main role of Victim was predictable. During the retreat Tara was also able to be reconciled with her father. She came to understand that once reconciled with him interiorly, as a woman free of resentment she could help her sick parent effectively.

(3) Peter the deformed, rejected child who found healing:

> When I was born, I was deformed. I had cleft lips so I could not take my mother's milk properly. Later I learned that because of this deformity my mother could not accept me. My father was a regular drunkard. He was mostly not home. When he was, he would often beat my mother. Towards me he was very strict, and I was afraid of him. As a small kid I remember always being hungry. Once I started going to school, the other children teased me because of my split lips. I was put into the hostel. I hated school life, though I studied well and showed real ability in karate, football, the national cadet corps training and in technical studies. During my high school days I sexually misused many boys and girls. At that time I didn't think it was wrong. Everyone in the hostel was acting the same way. "Blue" cinemas. pornographic photos, books and magazines were my constant companions. Whenever I drew close to anyone, I used them selfishly for my pleasure. I did this even with the girl I loved most. Now, after we have married, we have no children. I feel very lonely at times. I have a drinking habit and a bad temper. I know my wife has been sent by God. She loves me in spite of my bad habits. During this retreat the heavenly Father has helped me remove the hold these bad habits have had on me. Through a good confession and giving and receiving forgiveness I know I have a Father who loves me.

COMMENT: Peter came to realise in the IHR that his parents did not love each other. And so there was no real love in the family

DAY SIX : FORGIVING

either. It is understandable then that he went looking for affection and acceptance in ways he had learnt at school from his companions. This insight does not excuse Peter from the many injuries he committed against so many other people with his lust. But that insight helped him see that though as a young man he did evil things he was not by that fact an evil person. This is a distinction to remember. Otherwise, the shame and temptation to reject self that come with the beginning of repentance can be unbearable. In the retreat Peter experienced God's healing love for him. This came about through reconciliation both through the sacraments and through prayer by the retreat community. After the retreat he wrote to me saying that he realised he needs to come more closely to the Lord. He also learned how to pray and how to appreciate his wife. Lastly and most humbly, he described for me his desire for a child, "I have no strength to have a child of my own. But the Lord is my Father. God can heal me and give me a child."

* **HOLY HOUR:** There is some important personal work for each retreatant to do today. This is to make a double list of persons: (1) who have hurt us and (2) whom we have hurt. The holy hour will be an important help to compose this list. During it we will ask the Eucharistic Lord to walk back with us down the lanes of our lives, through every significant period: from conception, gestation, birth, and the first year of life, through pre-school and school years, through our work experience, through married years for the laity, and through religious and priestly years for religious and clerics. We pray to the Holy Spirit to help us remember when we were hurt and when we hurt others, knowingly or unknowingly, deliberately or undeliberately, the real hurts and the imagined ones. We want to become aware of them, accept them as our own responsibility and offer them to the Lord for healing. With the Lord we want to give and receive unconditional forgiveness. We want to be washed clean of anger and resentment, of guilt and shame and rage. It helps sometimes to have two animators to take turns with the successive stages of our lives. These animators meditatively move through each stage suggesting the possible situations in which we may either have been hurt or have given hurts to others. It also helps before this review of life begins for an animator to explain that

for the Lord there is no past or future. Everything is present, now. So, when we ask the Lord to heal and touch us and others, the hurtful event is present to Him, the Lord of History in whose hand is the wheel of time. He can and will transform the meaning of those painfilled events of our past. It also helps people to trust that mercifully the Lord's Spirit will not recall everything to us today--this would be too much. We will be reminded of those traumatic happenings for which God's grace has made us ready. Life is a pilgrimage. Sufficient for the day is the pain thereof!

EUCHARISTIC CELEBRATION: The biblical theme, pardon and forgiveness, is exceptionally rich. The choice of readings will be a matter of selecting from many possibilities those which are most relevant to this retreat community. A Mass for the Promotion of Harmony is suggested, using the first Eucharistic Prayer for Reconciliation. Readings: 1) Si (Ecclesiasticus) 27:30-28:1-5 or Jb 42:7-11 or Col 3:12-15; 2) Ps 41:7-13; 3) Mt 6:7-15.

* NIGHT COMMON SHARING: At this point of the retreat people are more than ready to share at night sessions. It is ideal to have a variety of persons give their witness, especially those who have not yet spoken. So the animator needs to state and to repeat the principle: "BE TO THE POINT, BE BRIEF, BE GONE!"

* TEAM EVALUATION: Animators of programmes often use a figure of speech from aviation. They speak of "getting off the ground". Just as the take-off of a plane is critical, so too for IHRs is the question whether each retreatant is into the retreat actively. It may be there is someone who is still "preparing for take-off". If this is so, an animator may respectfully enquire from the person/s whether counselling is desired. If it is, then the animating team will respectfully offer this service.

DAY SIX: FORGIVING

PRAYER FOR THE GRACE TO GIVE & RECEIVE FORGIVENESS

(For Day Six)

Abba, Father, Your Son Jesus tells me You are above all Merciful/
During this retreat I've come to feel my pains from yesterday/
My rejections and resentments stored up in some hidden part of me/
Yes, they're here! they're mine ! they hurt as fresh wounds do/

Jesus, mercy me, a selfbound soul, to let go, to give forgiveness/
Asking mercy, too, for many times I've struck hurts in near ones/
If there's any lesson You're more than clear about, it's this/
If I want healing mercy, then I've got to share the mercy given me/

Spirit of love and life divine, Soul of God's true children/
Grace me to forgive my "enemies"--everyone who has hurt me/
Grace me to ask that pardon I need for my own treacheries/
Fashion me more and more to be who I am in my Father's heart/

_____

DAY SEVEN

A TIME FOR HEALING: BY THANKING

Be at peace among yourselves......Make sure that people do not try to repay evil for evil; always aim at what is best for each other and for everyone. Always be joyful; pray constantly; and for all things give thanks; this is the will of God for you in Christ Jesus. (1 Th 5:14-18)

* **AIM OF THE DAY:** (a) To deal with our feelings of fears and shame; (b) to commit ourselves unconditionally to a eucharistic spirituality--of giving thanks always and everywhere for all tnings. In order to receive these gifts we want two other graces: (c) to let go of our proud, panic compulsion to control people and situations in order (d) to allow God to bring about the divine plan according to God's timetable, not ours.

* **MORNING PRAYER:** Ps 34 *("I will bless Yahweh at all times......')* This is an alphabetical wisdom psalm, partly thanksgiving and partly instruction about the different fortunes of good and evil persons. This song puts strong emphasis on a healthy fear of God-- the Hindu would express this holy reverence as *shraddhaa.* This psalm also distinguishes an unhealthy terror and shame from which God delivers devout souls: *"I seek Yahweh and he answers me, frees me from all my fears. Fix your gaze on Yahweh and your face will grow bright, you will never hang your head in shame"* (Ps 34:4-5).

* **MEDITATION:** Thanksgiving is an essential element of every authentic conversion. To experience christian gratitude deeply and permanently we need to understand some important differences, of which many people are not aware: e.g. the difference between holy and unholy fear, between healthy and unhealthy guilt or shame. These are issues which come within Day Seven's overall

DAY SEVEN : THANKING

theme of thanksgiving-at-all-times. These subjects find much place in our pilgrim experience. They are also seen in many gospel scenes. A suggested passage for today's meditation according to our theme is Jn 21: 1-23, the appearance on the shore of Tiberias, with special attention to Peter's sentiments of joyful gratitude and guilt, and how Jesus confronts his apostle with the truth-in-love.

* COMMON REFLECTION I-III: As the IHR progresses more and more time is devoted to personal sharing among retreatants, less and less time to common reflections by the animating staff. These brief presentations blend biblical and liturgical teaching with the witness of personal case studies.

Thanksgiving, Reflex Of Refined Humanity

We can say without exaggeration that thanksgiving is a reflex of a humanity that has been refined. All cultures, as far as I know, express gratitude, but they differ in how they do it. Expressing thanks is definitely culturally conditioned. For example, here in India many cultures express thanks largely non- verbally, through accepted signs and rituals. The fact that people of a certain culture do not say "thanks" does not mean that they are ungrateful or that they do not acknowledge gratitude as a positive value. Gratitude is, after all, a duty of all thinking people. Only a mentally sick person--or a senselessly proud, evil one-does not express gratitude. G.K. Chesterton states this in his own special style: "Unthinking, unthanking."

The Bible, History Of Thanksgiving

According to the bible, gratitude is a sure sign of authentic faith-conversion. Thanksgiving is a gift of the Spirit. It is also a duty When the faithful perceive God's gifts, they consider it a serious obligation for them to respond with appropriate praise and worship. Biblically the gift to God which is most pleasing is a sincere, joyful "sacrifice of thanksgiving". It is at the heart of living the truth-in-love, responding most rightly to God's free, generous gifts of love to us His beloved children. Faith and thanksgiving, therefore, go and grow together.

In the presence of the one, true, living God, if our first gesture as persons with faith is to prostrate ourselves in adoration, then our immediate second gesture is to stand up, raise our heads, our arms and our voices in a grateful shout of "Alleluia!" The greater the gift, the more the gratitude. We see this in the Bible from beginning to end. It is essential to sacred revelation's message to us of saving-truth. According to scripture between the All-Good Creator and creatures, who are truly *faithful,* there is an "essential exchange" (in Hebrew, *Baarak).* God continually graces his children with life, growth, and all gifts necessary for their fullness forever; and God's faithful family responds by acknowledging this divine generosity and goodness with thanksgiving, especially in a liturgical assembly. If we look at the 150 psalms, for example, we find not only an anthology of Old Testament spirituality but also a kind of primer of thanksgiving. With the full revelation of God's love coming to perfection in Jesus, the Old and New Testament revelation is, in fact, a history of maturing gratitude.

Growing Revelation, Growing Gratitude

As the process of revelation progresses step-by-step, so too does the quality of thanks. We know that divine revelation is in stages. There is a divinely patient, consistent pedagogy which God used to help His human family--at times, so foolish and slow to believe-- receive and properly appreciate precious, saving gifts. This divine pedagogy of revelation climaxes in Jesus Christ.

> *At many moments in the past and by many means, God spoke to our ancestors through the prophets, but in our time, the final days, he has spoken to us in the person of his Son, whom he appointed Their of all things and through whom he made the ages.* (Heb 1: 1- 2)

DAY SEVEN : THANKING

Jesus, The Man Of Perfect Gratitude

It is with Jesus Christ that human gratitude achieves its highest, total, and permanent expression. In his very person Jesus is above all the "Man of Thanks". In all four gospel accounts we can trace out his unique habit of giving thanks for everything, always, everywhere. The greatest and most permanent of these acts is his supreme Thanksgiving Sacrifice expressed at the Last Supper and on Calvary. Through this sacrificial meal, Jesus sealed the New and Everlasting Covenant between God and the human family. It's not surprising that inspired writers of the first christian century use a new word for this most central act of christian thanksgiving. They used the Greek word <u>Eucharist</u>. It is employed over 60 times in the New Testament.

As for the Bible so for the Liturgy, too, Christ's Eucharist is at the very centre of all life and growth. This is shown throughout 2.000 years of the Church's history.

> *The liturgy is the summit toward which the activity of the Church is directed; it is also the fount from which all her power flows. For the goal of apostolic endeavour is that all who are made sons/daughters of God by faith and baptism should come together to praise God in the midst of his Church, to take part in the Sacrifice and to eat the Lord's Supper.*

(Vatican II's Constitution on the Sacred Liturgy, 10)

The Liturgical Law Of Thanks

Lex orandi, lex credendi! The rule of prayer is the norm of belief. From the earliest centuries of the christian era the Church's eucharistic action began with the following dialogue between celebrant and worshipping assembly:

Celebrant: Lift up your hearts!
Assembly: We lift them up to the Lord.

151

> Celebrant: Let us give thanks to the Lord our God!
> Assembly: It is right to give him thanks and praise.
> Celebrant: Father, All-Powerful and Ever--living God, we do well always and everywhere to give You thanks.

The New Code of Church Law published in 1983 describes briefly and beautifully what this great act of thanksgiving means to Christians:

> The Most Holy Eucharist is the most august sacrament, in which Christ the Lord himself is contained, offered and received, and by which the Church constantly lives and grows. The Eucharistic Sacrifice, the memorial of the death and resurrection of the Lord, in which the sacrifice of the cross is perpetuated over the centuries, is the summit and the source of all Christian worship and life; it signifies and effects the unity of the people of God and achieves the building up of the Body of Christ. The other sacraments and all the ecclesiastical works of the apostolate are closely related to the Holy Eucharist and are directed to it. (Can. 897)

As I stop and think of the people who have most influenced my life, they are those who have been most loving, most truthful and exceptionally thankful. Let's turn now to some of these grateful people and see how they lived their lives with constant thanks.

The Carpenter Who Built His House Upon Gratitude

One of most memorable people I have known was a simple-living village carpenter. I first came to know him well as he and his wife were celebrating their fiftieth wedding anniversary. Surrounded by eleven grown children of their own--and numerous grandchildren--he and his wife renewed their wedding vows at Mass in the village church in which practically his whole life he had ministered as a

DAY SEVEN : THANKING

choir member. This golden couple celebrated with a marriage banquet for all their family in their ancestral home that had been built entirely by this man. Located in an almost entirely christian village, not only was this house a labour of love, it was a monument to this carpenter's faith. On the roof of his home, he had painted the words in large letters for all passersby to see: "ALL WHO ENTER HERE ARE WELCOMED IN THE HOLY NAME OF JESUS!" As a gift to each of their children, he and his wife sent a handwritten letter. It was a touching expression of two happy parents, of their deep thanks to God and to their children for half-a-century of married-family life, that had by no means been always easy. On one of the walls of this carpenter's house he had placed a prayer written in his native dialect. Here it is in translation. To me it sums up his remarkably happy, holy life:

THANK YOU !

Thank You for this lovely morning/ Thank You for this new/born day/
Thank You that I may entrust all my cares to You/
Thank You for all good friends/ Thank You for everyone/
Thank You I can give forgiveness even to my greatest foe/
Thank You for my livelihood/ Thank you for ev'ry little joy/
Thank You for all that is bright and happy and for music, too/
Thank You for what sometimes made me sad and for each good word/
Thank You that Your loving hand still guides me
where e're I am/
Thank You for the gift of Your Spirit so to understand Your Word/
Thank You that You extend Your love to all folks near and far/
Thank You that Your loving kindness knows no bounds/
Thank You that I will hold fast to it/
Thank You, yes, Lord, I want to thank You I can give
You thanks/

A TIME FOR HEALING

Thanksgiving In Hunger And Thirst

In my pilgrim efforts to become a grateful person I shall not forget what happened to me one very hot summer's day in 1980. With a companion I had set out at 7 a.m. to be with a sick person who was in urgent need of prayer. Our journey was on foot through a sparse forest. We had been trudging three hours when I felt sharp hunger, thirst and weakness in my legs. I knew if I didn't take some nourishment quickly I would probably collapse from the mounting, intense heat. With few signs of civilisation in this jungle spot I felt we were "in the middle of no where". What to do? I remember next surrendering the situation in a trust that didn't come easily or feel good. I prayed something like this: "Lord, thanks, that I can give You my tired body and hungry feelings. I know I can get help from You. Do something soon!" This prayer in my heart was no sooner finished than I saw three green plums on the ground just in front of me. With a rush of kid's joy I picked them up like some priceless treasures. I dusted them off, offered one to my companion and was about to take a bite into mine when I noticed we were standing directly under a plum tree, full of ripe fruit! I next noticed a shepherd boy grazing his sheep nearby. With help of his stick I was able to collect a good number of plums. They were delicious! As I devoured them I knew the Lord had heard at least part of my prayer. So I reminded Him that we were still very thirsty: "Lord, thanks for the plums. And thanks again that I can entrust this thirst into Your hands." We continued our journey. Within about a quarter-of-an-hour we came to a house. I saw a lady was on the front verandah; she was about to throw away some water in a glass. I called out to her to save the contents for us. Instead of that, she drew some fresh water and served us. We had plenty of clean, cold water to slake our thirst. And my strength revived for the rest of that journey.

I have thought back many times to this incident and others like it. From these faith-experiences I know within my heart that when I surrender a situation with trustful thanks to the Lord, He arranges mini miracles for me in a most wonderful way.

DAY SEVEN :   THANKING

Trustful Thanks Work Wonders

In the New Testament thanksgiving is connected closely with confessing faith, giving praise, and glorifying God. In his very attractive little books Rev. Merlin Carothers has brought out clearly how this integration of faith, praise and thanks allows the Lord to work wonders of his love. These mini-marvels nurture people's faith, happiness and salvation. Carothers' writings have helped one of my friends and confreres very much to develop a eucharistic spirituality for daily life. Since beginning this Way of Thanks, he has had a number of very striking experiences that cannot be explained as just "lucky" coincidences. I asked him to describe a few of these happenings for me in writing. Here are three short accounts which he recently sent:

(1) Stolen Luggage And Surrendering Gratitude:

> If you will excuse the play on words, my journey of offering thanks for everything began on a train ride when all my luggage had been stolen. This is what happened. I was in Khadwa, Madhya Pradesh, conducting a retreat. Because there were only a few participants I found plenty of time for myself to read three books, which someone had given me. They were written by Merlin Carothers: *Prison To Praise, Praise Works,* and *Answers To Praise.* The scriptural passages and personal examples of how Carothers lived God's Word really convinced me that here was a very attractive and powerful way of confessing Jesus as the Lord of every circumstance. What also caught my attention was that this attitude of faith helped foster inner peace and joy in circumstances where many people erupt into fear, anger and frustration. Retreat over. I boarded my train for Patna--some 24 hours away. Opposite me in the second class compartment was a very, very large lady, surrounded by four small children, pots, pans, fire wood, and enough food to feed a small army. She and her family were going on pilgrimage to Ranchi. She was not only of generous porportions; she talked the whole day and late into the night almost non-stop. By eleven-thirty p.m. I was thoroughly tired out. I decided to go

155

to sleep, in spite of the fact that we were scheduled soon to arrive at Moghulsarai. It has a well merited title of being a *chor bazaar*–a market for thieves. I figured this matriarch would continue to be on guard-- probably talking throughout the night--so I had no fear of losing anything. I fell into a deep sleep and awoke only around 6 a.m. It was then full daylight and we were far beyond Moghulsarai, heading towards Patna, my destination. Practically as soon as I opened my eyes, this lady opposite me shouted in Hindi, 'Where is your luggage?" I glanced under the seat and saw that my suitcase was gone. At that instant I remembered the words I had read so often in Carothers' books from 1 Th 5: 18, "For all things give thanks!" And for a split second I began to "reason" with God: "But, Lord, *this* is too much!" And the scriptural command came back again even more forcefully, "For ALL things give thanks!" That settled it! I made my decision, looked up and said to the lady, *"Prabhoo kee Jai!"* (Praise be to the Lord!). Her mouth dropped open, and she asked me to repeat what I had said. I did and added a word from the Book of Job, *"The Lord gave, the Lord has taken back."* (Jb 1:21) This sentence completely flabbergasted the woman. She called her children to attention and repeated to them what I had said. Then she asked me what was in my luggage. I mentioned a few things and then fell into silence. "Here I am," I thought, "I have no ticket. No clothes except what I'm wearing--undershirt and pyjama pants. No money. And still I'm calm and not in the least worried. In fact I have rarely felt so happy and strong. This is a brand new experience!" I very much liked the interior feed-back and recognised it as coming from God's Spirit. I hadn't felt like thanking God but deep within me I knew I should and so I did--refusing to pay attention to some very angry thoughts that raced through my mind. Once at Patna Junction I carefully avoided the ticket man at the exit gate. Making my way home I soon forgot about the whole incident. But two days later I received a telegram from the Ranchi Railway Police telling me that my luggage was with them and that I should arrange to pick it up. This was a totally unexpected invitation. Another surprise was to identify the suspect

DAY SEVEN : THANKING

thief. The train on which my belongings were stolen was going to Calcutta. The thief who took my luggage had to detrain at Patna with me and then that night take an express to Ranchi. Who was going to Ranchi that same night? The large lady who was my next berth neighbour! At this discovery I laughed heartily. I also learned a lesson about what to do when things turn "impossible"--surrender them if not with uderstanding then at least with thankful trust to the Lord.

(2) A Timely Train Reservation With Two Guardian Angels:

The words of scripture are simple and uncompromising: the will of God for us in Christ Jesus is to be always joyful, to pray constantly and for everything to give thanks. To live these words demands that we be obviously "fools for Christ's sake" (1 Co 4:10). I have rarely felt so "foolish" as one night in the Patna railway station. A member of our pastoral centre's staff had received an express telegram calling her home to her mother, who was seriously sick. This Sister received the message in the evening and she wanted to leave immediately, despite the fact that she had no reservation for this journey which would take her three nights in the train, Patna to Cochin. I and another staff member took her to the station to catch a 10 p.m. Express for Calcutta. This train was always very crowded; in the unreserved section it was usually standing room only. As the three of us waited, we heard an announcement that this train was running one hour late. An hour passed. Eleven p.m., we were all tired. Then came another announcement: her train was now running two hours late! The prospect was that this Express would come well past midnight. I felt the urge to be "foolish": to ask my two companions to join me in thanking the Lord that we could entrust this journey into His hands. The other two looked at me with blank faces and kept silent during my prayer. Once it was over I felt difficulty keeping my eyes from sleep, so I decided to walk up and down the platform. I had gone one length when I heard an "hello" with my name called out. It was a Jesuit novice I knew; with him there were two young men. He introduced them as his brothers. I told him of the plight we were in. His answer amazed me. "Father, I was expecting *three* brothers to visit me. At the last moment, one could not come. So I have three tickets-with-reservations all the way to South India. Sister can use the extra reservation." Our "foolish" prayer of surrendering-thanks had been heard better than anything I could imagine! Not only did Sister get a gift reservation but she was given a surprise bonus besides: two strong guardian angels, to look after her needs and to converse with her in her mother tongue!

(3) Broken Bones Bless The Lord:

In October, 1983, I was conducting a ten day retreat-seminar for church leaders, when I broke my right femur by slipping on some water and falling across a steel door frame. The sudden slip and the blinding pain of three broken hip bones slammed into me as nothing in my life. The hurt was so extreme I thought my heart would stop any second. Surprisingly, the only words that came to me were, "Thank you, Jesus!" Why I kept repeating only these words, I don't fully know. All I remember about that time before I arrived at the hospital and was given pain killer is two things: (a) I was tempted to scream in blind fear and (b) somehow I realised that the Lord was very close to me. This "accident" was the beginning of a long juorney. It put me into a hospital bed for over four months and onto crutches for about a year. It was also a time of very painful and yet very memorable learnings. Though I had been a Jesuit religious for 38 years and a priest for 24, I still had not learned many basic lessons, spiritually and emotionally--like not taking for granted God's gifts of health such as standing, walking, running and moving about freely. These and so many other graces are so precious and wonderful, still I didn't appreciate them until they were suddenly withdrawn from me. Well, to make a long story a little shorter, blessing the Lord for my broken bones brought me plenty of choice graces, too many to enumerate here. Not the least of these was to experience unforgettably my own weakness. Later, I was to read in the life of St. Ignatius of Loyola that a favourite aunt of his one day remonstrated with young

DAY SEVEN : THANKING

Ignatius who was then a boy, "Inigo, you will never get any sense until someone breaks one of your legs!" That is exactly what happened to him years later at Pamplona. From those broken bones he did learn some "sense". And so did I. Thanks to God, I'm still learning.

* **HOLY HOUR :** Today it is suggested that the retreatants spend an hour of thanksgiving. It may help some to put into writing names of persons and places/events for which they are particularly grateful. This record of graces is very biblical and liturgical. When the covenant was renewed in Old Testament days ritually there was an historical prologue, which enumerated the major graces which God had given to Israel. As salvation history progressed, this prologue of thanks became longer and longer. In the Preface and Eucharistic Prayer each day during Mass we recall with gratitude the saving events of Christ's Paschal Exodus. So, each retreatant is encouraged to write down with thanks the saving acts in their own personal salvation history.

* **EUCHARISTIC CELEBRATION:** For this theme of thanking a votive Mass of the Holy Name of Jesus is recommended. The second eucharistic prayer for Reconciliation may be used. Suggested readings are: 1) 2 Co 4: 7-15); 2) Ps 136--this litany of thanksgiving is the Great Hallel; parts of it may be used; 3) Lk 10: 17-24.

* **NIGHT COMMON SHARING :** In keeping with the day's focus, the animator guides personal sharings while interspersing songs of thanks and praise. The difference between thanks and praise may also be pointed out. In prayers of thanksgiving we acknowledge that God has given us so many blessings; in praise, however, we thank God for God: Father, Son, Spirit. In this sense thanks culminates in praise and worship.

* **TEAM EVALUATION :** As usual.

A TIME-FOR HEALING

PRAYER FOR THE GRACE OF GRATITUDE
(For Day Seven)

Abba, Only heart's eye of faith can see the world full of wonders/
Mini-maxi miracles of rainbowed, crisscrossed curves of
    symmetry/
Planetary furniture breathtaking, spinning galaxies through my
    mind/
Father, cut the knot of petty, tongue-tied ingratitude binding me/
All my life I don't want to be miserly ungrateful into eternity/
Child of Your faithful, tender love forever what more can I ask/

Jesus, teaching thanks with ev'ry tiny piece of bread and breath/
"Ev'rything is possible for You, My *Abba!*" Cried You on Calvary/
Gardens of Gethsemane, dusty village roads and city streets/
Grateful Son for little boy's gift, tiffin box of fish and crumbs/
Bread and wine at Thursday's feast, Body/Blood for Friday's fast/
Feeding centuries of children, youth, adults, and wizened heads/
Quiet, hidden, total Self-Gift, Love loves to serve till it hurts/
Let me, Lord, try at least to match Your gift singing gratefully/

Spirit' powering the martyrs young and old to praise and thank/
Midst furnaces of fire, passions lit by lust, and raging beasts/
Tortures conjured up by jealousies, satanic hate and wounded
    pride/
Choirs chanting ev'ry second to their Lord: *"Koti-koti*
    Dhanyabaad!"
Grant to me a grateful heart, a spirit generous to see God's gifts/
Offering a worthy sacrifice of thanks of all I am and my yet to be/

DAY EIGHT

A TIME FOR HEALING: BY FOLLOWING

> *"If anyone wants to be a follower of mine, let him renounce himself and take up his cross every day and follow me. Anyone who wants to save his life will lose it; but anyone who loses his life for my sake, will save it. What benefit is it to anyone to win the whole world and forfeit or lose his very self?"* (Lk 9:23-25)

* AIM OF THE DAY: (a) to renew our baptism's consecration, which is the most important and solemn of fundamental options, to follow Jesus as our Way till the end of our pilgrimage; (b) to realise that christian faith-commitment means a life-long, deepening surrender unconditionally to our Saviour. This implies progressively, patiently putting on the mind and heart of Christ so as to be more and more conformed to His life--not just His Joyful Mysteries, but through the Sorrowful Mysteries to Jesus' GLorious Mysteries of Life-after-life; (c) to understand by felt-experience that growth in faithful following of Jesus can only be achieved within a community-of-the-Spirit.

* MORNING PRAYER: Ps 1 *("How blessed is anyone who rejects the advice of the wicked and does not take a stand in the path that sinners tread......")* This opening psalm is a meditation upon "The Two Ways"--that of the evil and good. Together with Psalm 2 it sums up the whole moral message of the Psalter. Our Lord certainly was aware of this when He described Himself as the Way, Truth and Life (see Jn 14;6).

* MEDITATION: The final step in any authentic conversion is unconditional commitment to follow the Lord every day of life's pilgrimage. Today's theme, then, climaxes our reflections on christian conversion. Day eight corresponds to the Election of an Ignatian retreat. Luke 9:23-26 is very apt for this day's opening meditation since it is about the condition of following Christ. It focuses squarely on the disciple's response to the Lord's total self-gift to her/him.

* **COMMON REFLECTIONS I-III :** As on Day Seven, these reflections leave more time for personal sharing in teams. Animators, therefore, do well to keep their presentations brief. They will seek to offer such biblical themes as (a) *following of Christ,* (b) *christian discipliship,* and (c) *faithfullness.* It helps also to give examples of witnesses who have successfully lived these gospel ideals.

From Committment To Confidence

I'm not a bold person by nature. Far from it. Whenever I read the story of Saul's conversion in Acts 9 I'm attracted to the character of Ananias in Damascus who was sent by the Lord to Saul --like a sheep into the roaring lion's den. My version of this story is that Ananias was trembling inside and outside as he approached Saul, the Persecutor from Tarsus who had hunted down and jailed so many christian disciples. But despite his fears and anxieties, Ananias did his job with a mysterious, bold confidence given him by the Lord's Spirit. This calm courage in Christ's committed disciples is seen throughout Acts of the Apostles. It is fruit of the Spirit's action in those who have generously surrendered themselves and their lives to the Lord. This apostolic boldness and powerful confidence in following the Lord through very dangerous circumstances surprises even those to whom these gifts are given (see Act 12, the account of Peter's miraculous deliverance). Let me describe one of the most surprising journeys of confidence on which the Lord has led me.

A Boat Ride I'll Never Forget

In November 1987 I was in Bangladesh conducting a series of retreats, both for laity and members of the national charismatic service team. The whole trip was put under a cloud even before it began. While still in India I read in newspapers that Bangladesh was threatened with public demonstrations during the very days my retreats were scheduled. I decided not to cancel those retreats but

DAY EIGHT : FOLLOWING

to surrender the whole project into the Lord's hands. It was for Him that I was going, He would have to take care of me. I wasn't disappointed in this trust. Everything went well during the whole time of my retreats. The "fun" began when I wanted to return to India. I was scheduled to fly out of Bangladesh on November 30. But since serious trouble was predicted for that day, I decided to move my flight date up to the 27th. I was in the hinterland and had to make a boat trip to Dacca's International Airport on the 24th. A total curfew had been declared until 2 p.m., which was the exact time of my ship's scheduled departure. How was I and my sister companion to get to the docks during a police curfew? It didn't take me long to recognise the circumstances as another "impossible" situation in which I knew the Lord wanted me to give the whole thing to Him confidently and to keep myself in peace. I made this offering as we began our journey towards the dock area. Without too much delay we found a cycle rickshawman who was willing to "run" the curfew in order to get us to our boat on time. On the way to the jetty the police did not give us any difficulties. Both of us were silent that whole journey. We kept looking at our watches and urgently praising the Lord, reminding Him that we had to make that boat. When we arrived, however, we could see our vessel already well out into the harbour. It had left without us! Some Muslim fishermen, who were sitting in their canoes, saw our plight and began shouting to the ship's captain to wait. Hearing their cries, he cut his engine. Then these goodhearted sailors told us to jump from the dock down into their small canoe. Here we were, two sisters standing on the pier. Fully eleven feet down was this small canoe, bobbing up and down in the waves, and we were supposed to jump down there. Just like that! I was scared stiff. The first thing that came to my mind was that this was my final act in life. For a moment I didn't know what to do. I remember praying spontaneously, "Lord, I praise and thank You for allowing me to die in this water." (I wasn't joking. From an early childhood experience, I was always deathly afraid of water and small boats.) Well, the next thing I did was jump into the waiting arms of one of the sailors, who caught me gently and firmly. Encouraged by this success my companion followed with another "circus leap" safely and we headed for our waiting boat. When we reached the ship, its captain let down a rope and hauled us up to the three storey high ocean steamer. For the whole journey we sat on the sunny deck, two Sisters shivering in the November chill, suffering from mild shock but very thankful to God that He had saved us from what we understood as an encounter with death. When I arrived at Dacca I discovered that because of a national curfew my flight was to be the last plane out of the country that day. (As it turned out, the national emergency lasted several days.)

Arriving in Calcutta's airport three days ahead of my scheduled flight home, I learned that there was an Indian Airlines plane for Patna in just two hours. To get onto that flight I had to travel into the city's airline reservations' office, change my booking date and then return to the airport in time. So, I walked from the international arrival lounge to the national departure area to catch a city bus. There I met a lovely Bengali lady who was my nextdoor neighbour in Patna. She had just arrived at the airport with some relatives. I explained my situation. She quickly obliged by sending me into Calcutta in her own family car-- which was equipped with air-conditioning and stereo music besides. I went back and forth from the airport in record time, and as I sat in the plane that afternoon heading towards Patna I had no difficulty thanking and praising the Lord for the way He had taken such good care of me during the whole journey, but especially that day. It had started early morning in a curfew-bound back-country of Bangladesh. Within twelve hours I had travelled by rickshaw, canoe, ocean steamer, international jet and luxury car. Now I was heading back to Patna by Boeing three days ahead of schedule, safe and sound. It was a trip I'll never forget.

Faithful Lives And Apostolic Fruitfulness

The spirit of independence is in the air and it is surely a great value. Freedom, democracy, self-rule, initiative, creativity, free-trade, open market. These are the media buzz words, which are front page vocabulary for media around the world. The spirit behind these words can mean courage to be free from oppressions of all sorts. But there is another kind of independence which negates obedience and devalues fidelity both to God and those to whom we

DAY EIGHT: FOLLOWING

own allegiance. Today permanent commitment is not popular. "Doing your own thing" is.

Unhealthy independence and failure to keep life-long commitments are at the opposite pole from Christian fidelity. The baptismal covenant means commitment to imitating God's own incorruptible fidelity, his faithful love. The Christian vocation is a consecration by the Spirit's anointing to disciples, following Christ as Lord and being conformed more and more to his paschal pilgrimage. Jesus demands this obedience to the Spirit in faithful imitation of Him, our Master and Lord. He, not I, is the driver of my life. He, not I, knows the best--*and only*--road map of my life's mission. I do not know what may be coming my way or whom I shall be meeting today. He tells me, *"There is no need to be afraid: you are more than many sparrows .. And yet not one is forgotten in God's sight."* (Lk 12:7,6) Awareness that we are doing our best to be fully faithful to the Spirit's guidance brings peace and apostolic fruitfulness.

I used to be anxious about the future, how I would meet certain people and cope with difficult situations. Since I unconditionally surrendered to follow Jesus as my Lord and All, I experience that my life has changed a lot. I'm confident that Jesus is in charge not only of myself and of my every desire but also of every person, every situation. Even if on some days everything seems to be going wrong, deep down there is a peaceful conviction that He will put everything right according to His way and His timing. What scripture says I have seen to be literally true, though at the time I may not have been conscious of it: *"We are well aware that God works with those who love Him, those who have been called in accordance with His purpose, AND TURNS EVERYTHING TO THEIR GOOD."* (Ac 8:28-29)

The key to apostolic fruitfulness, I think, is in this obedient following of the Lord. Some time ago Mother Teresa of Calcutta was being interviewed by media people. After she responded to a question, a newspaperman commented, "But Mother, that is not efficient!" Her answer was right to the target. "The Lord called me," she said, "Not to be first of all 'efficient' but to be obedient to Him!"

A TIME FOR HEALING

In my own life 1981 was crucial for me. I was still relatively new to this ministry of healing and retreats. Communication with my own sisters was not all that good as I would have wished. I had to go through much misunderstanding within my community. I reconsecrated myself to the Lord, renewing faith in Him as Lord of my life. Not long after that renewal both I and my situation changed. As though there had been no problems I found that no one and no situation could disturb my peace. "Out of the blue" I was invited to Rome to participate in the International Leadership Convention among the Catholic Charismatics. During that stay I was offered the rare opportunity to explain to my religious superiors what the Renewal meant for religious life. On so many other occasions clearly the Lord's hand was evident to arrange everything beautifully amidst confusion, sorrow, and miscommunication. My growing certainty is that serious, sustained efforts to follow the Lord closely leads to apostolic courage and fruitfulness. Could it be otherwise?

> *"As you received Jesus as Lord and Christ, now live your lives in him, be rooted in him and built on him, held firm by the faith you have been taught, and overflowing with thanksgiving."* (Col 2:6-7)

Living our daily lives consciously rooted in Him, we draw all our strength from Him--as branches from its vine (Jn 15). We can and do experience this parable of Jesus as perfectly accurate. Being His unconditionally, when we ask for His grace He answers because He is most faithful-- *"he cannot disown his own self."*

Following The Lord In A Twelve Step Programme

The grace we ask throughout Day Eight is to commit ourselves to following Jesus ever more closely. We ask this because we desire to be continually formed according to God's eternal plan for us of holiness, wholeness and wellness. We also ask the grace to be convinced that life-long fidelity to Christ's call is impossible unless we are constantly encouraged within a community that is of-the-

DAY EIGHT : FOLLOWING

Spirit: a group of persons who are seriously committed to living God's will for each of them one day at a time.

On the world scene there are millions of people who are following what has come to be called the "Twelve Step Programme" of recovery. This regimen is extraordinarily successful in helping people who are striving for inner healing and freedom from addictions of many kinds: alcohol, drugs, overeating, sexual disorders, gambling, etc. These recovery groups are not a substitute for religious affiliation, though they believe firmly in a personal God. They are not allied with any one religious denomination or sect. They are not politically affiliated. They do not engage in controversy of any sort nor endorse nor oppose ideologies and causes. All of these therapeutic communities follow the wise guidance and proven principles of the Twelve Steps and Twelve Tradition in order to be healed of destructive addictions and to lead peaceful, productive, healthy lives. These steps and traditions have been adopted for different purposes from Alcoholic Anonymous, which is now over half a century old and successfully established around the world. I wish here briefly to draw attention of IHR participants to another 12 Step Programme which is called "Co-dependents Anonymous" (CoDA). I do so because I believe we who seek inner healing have much to learn from CoDA's experience as a witness to commitment.

What Is Co-Dependency?

In its International Service publication Co-Depandents Anonymous describes itself this way:

> "......a fellowship of men and women whose common problem is an inability to maintain functional relationships. We share with one another in the hopes of solving our common problem and helping others to recover. The only requirement for membership is a desire for healthy and fulfilling relationships with others and ourselves. . .Most of us have been searching for ways to overcome the dilemmas of the conflicts in our relationships and our childhoods. Many of us were raised in families where addictions existed--some of us were not. In either case, we have found in each of our lives that co-de-

pendency is a most deeply-rooted, compulsive behaviour and that it is born out of our sometimes moderately, sometimes extremely dysfunctional family systems. We have each experienced in our own ways the painful trauma of the emptiness of our childhood and relationships throughout our lives. We attempted to use others--our mates, our friends and even our children, as our sole source of identity, value and well-being and as a way of trying to restore within us the emotional losses from our childhoods. Our histories may include other powerful addictions which at times we have to use to cope with our co-dependency. We have all learned to survive life, but in CoDA we are learning to live life. Through applying the Twelve Steps and principles found in CoDA to our daily life and relationships, both present and past, we can experience a new freedom from our self-defeating lifestyles. It is an individual growth process. Each of us is growing at our own pace and will continue to do so as we remain open to God's will for us on a daily basis. Our sharing is our way of identification and helps us to free the emotional bonds of our past and the compulsive control of our present. No matter how traumatic your past or despairing your present may seem, there is hope for a new day in the programme of Co-dependents Anonymous. No longer do you need to rely on others as a power greater than yourself. May you instead find here a new strength within to be that which God intended--Precious and Free."[1]

Perhaps no other author has written more widely and more popularly about Codependent than Melody Beattie. Her first work was entitled *Codependent No More* (Harper & Row, Publishers, San Francisco, 1987). Its sub-title is indicative of what Codependency is: *How To Stop Controlling Others And Start Caring For Yourself*. In chapter three of this bestselling book Beattie catalogues a number of definitions on Codependency by specialists. Among them are the following:

---

[1] BY PERMISSION OF CO-DEPENDENTS ANNONYMOUS, INC., P.O. BOX 33577, PHEONIX, ARIZONA 85067-3577

DAY EIGHT : FOLLOWING

* "An emotional, psychological, and behavioural condition that develops as a result of an individual's prolonged exposure to, and practice of, a set of oppressive rules--rules which prevent the open expression of feeling as well as the direct discussion of personal and interpersonal problems." (Robert Subby)

* "Those self-defeating, learned behaviours or character defects that result in a diminished capacity to initiate or to participate in loving relationships." (Earnie Larsen)

* "A codependent person is one who has let another person's behaviour affect him or her, and who is obsessed with controlling that person's behaviour." (M. Beattie)

Since Codependency has been identified as a serious and widespread human problem only relatively recently, perhaps the best understanding of it comes from descriptions of how it affects people who are afflicted with it. Beattie lists fourteen characteristics of Codependency. This is not to say that all of these symptoms will be equally present in every codependent. Nor is it to state that these are its only manifestations. Here is a short summary paraphrase of what Miss Beattie presents more at length with plenty of examples:

(1) CARETAKING: codependents become so preoccupied with another person's behaviour, with what he/she thinks, feels, and needs, that they neglect an appropriate care of their own selves.

(2) LOW SELF-WORTH: although they hunger for acceptance and love, codependents regularly discount themselves and other people's praise and sincere compliments of them. In their heart of hearts they do not believe others love or appreciate them, because they do not appreciate or love themselves.

(3) REPRESSION: due to shame and unhealthy guilt, codependents suppress their own inner life, their views, values and feelings, undervaluing them as unimportant. Codependents avoid intimacy, fearing to remove a rigid mask of "self-control". They choose rather not to let themselves and close friends see their real selves.

A TIME FOR HEALING

(4) OBSESSION: codependents are compulsive, suspicious worriers, especially abour others' behaviour and problems.

(5) CONTROLLING: because of very painful experiences of living with a person who was dysfunctional and sometimes out of control, codependendents over-react by consciously or unconsciously trying to control people and situations, fearful to let them unfold and blossom spontaneously. This results in anger and frustration for everyone concerned.

(6) DENIAL: codependents both fear and deny problems along with the strong feelings connected with them. Treating such difficulties as though they did not exist, codependents often become workaholics. So much energy is spent avoiding the real issues in their lives that codependents feel drained and depressed; they may often get sick and at the same time wonder why.

(7) DEPENDENCY: codependents seek their own happiness not inside but outside themselves in the care of some dysfunctional person/s. Their emotional centre of gravity, so to speak, is outside themselves. In this process of overcaring, their own identity and self-esteem are built upon signs of approval from those for whom they compulsively give their lives. These "proofs of love" are often deceiving, defective or totally absent.

(8) POOR COMMUNICATION: codependents are typically people-pleasers. They do not speak what they think is true but what they judge the other person wants to hear. Lying is frequently a cover-up to protect those on whom they are dependent. When they want to say "no", they regularly say "yes"--so as not to hurt others' feelings, while disregarding their own.

(9) WEAK BOUNDARIES: shifting from being overtolerant to completely intolerant, codependents often feel vulnerable, manipulated and victimised. They are easily imposed upon. Others superficially interpret this trait in codependents as due to their good-naturedness, when in reality they may be seething with anger inside.

DAY EIGHT : FOLLOWING

(10) LACK OF TRUST: having been misunderstood and betrayed so often, at a deep-down level despite language to the contrary, codependents find it very difficult to trust themselves, others and, yes, even God, who they feel has given up on them as "hopeless cases".

(11) ANGER: fear, shame and anger are frequently experienced by codependents. Yet, they are often in a bind: they feel threatened and guilty about acknowledging that they have strong negative feelings. So the anger remains and increases because it is never allowed to surface or to be faced squarely.

(12) SEX PROBLEMS: married or unmarried, codependents have serious difficulties emotionally acknowledging that there is such a thing as a healthy, positive view towards sex. They often confuse love and sex, sex and intimacy. Paradoxically they can both exaggerate the importance of sex and dismiss it as utterly repulsive.

(13) MISCELLANEOUS CONTRADICTIONS: serious, permanent confusion is also characteristic of many codependents. They can quickly shift from being overly responsible to being totally irresponsible. They can be both lethargically passive and violently aggressive, impulsive and also indecisive.

(14) PROGRESSIVE: if alcoholism can be terminal, so too can codependency in its later stages. Left to itself, codependency is not "solved with time". It does not go away but grows in intensity, leaving the codependent increasingly depressed, disturbed and dysfunctional. It can and does make the codependent vulnerable to other addictions, violence and possibly suicide--deliberate or "accidental".

Sample Outline Of A CoDA Weekly Meeting

The purpose of presenting reflections on Codependency on the eighth day of our IHR is twofold: (a) while being at the root of many of our inner healing problems, Codependency can be a big block on our road to healing; (b) as Christians committed to our own pilgrimage towards holiness and wholeness, we can learn much from CoDA's programme of healing and recovery. The 12 Steps of Alcoholics Anonymous, of which CoDA's Programme is an adaptation, have been extraordinarily successful for over fifty years with people. The reason for this success is in the wisdom of its spiritual principles and in the commitment of its many members-- both as individuals and as communities. CoDA's serious determination is evident from an outline of a typical weekly meeting.

(a) Opening: after the meeting is called to order the first agenda is recitation by all the members together of the Serenity Prayer :

> God, Grant me the Serenity/
> To accept the things I cannot change/
> Courage to change the things I can/
> And the Wisdom to know the difference/

(b) The person who has volunteered to conduct the meeting welcomes everyone. He/she requests people who are at the meeting for the first time and out-of-town CoDA visitors to introduce themselves by their first names. Anyone in the group who has during the past week celebrated a CoDA "birthday" (anniversary of membership in CoDA), is asked to make this happy event known. Then starting with the chairperson everyone introduces themselves. This done in several ways: e.g. (1) "I'm Janet, I'm a recovering codependent," (2) "I'm Jim, I'm codependent," or simply (3) "I'm Al" (Mary, John, Helen, etc.) and the group responds together acknowledging the person (e.g. "Hi, Al!").

(c) The purpose and meaning of CoDA is then read out. A central place in this presentation is recitation of CoDA's TWELVE STEPS.[1]

1. We admitted we were powerless over others--that our lives had become unmanageable.

2. Came to believe that a power greater than ourselves could restore us to sanity.

DAY EIGHT: FOLLOWING

3. Made a decision to turn our will and our lives over to the care of God as we understood God.

4. Made a searching and fearless moral inventory of ourselves.

5. Admitted to God, to ourselves, and to another human being the exact nature of our wrongs.

6. Were entirely ready to have God remove all these defects of character.

7. Humbly asked God to remove our shortcomings.

8. Made a list of all persons we had harmed, and became willing to make amends to them all.

9. Made direct amends to such people wherever possible, except when to do so would injure them or others.

10. Continued to take personal inventory and when we were wrong promptly admitted it.

11. Sought through prayer and meditation to improve our conscious contact with God as we understood God, praying only for knowledge fo God's will for us and the power to carry that out.

12. Having had a spiritual awakening as the result of these steps, we tried to carry this message to other co-dependents, and to practice these principles in all our affairs.

After these steps are read. THE TWELVE TRADITIONS OF CO-DEPENDENTS ANONYMOUS are also read.

1. Our common welfare should come first; personal recovery depends upon CoDA unity.

2. For our group purpose there is but one ultimate authority--a loving higher power as expressed to our group conscience. Our leaders are but trusted servants; they do not govern.

1 & 2 BY PERMISSION OF CO-DEPENDENTS ANNONYMOUS, AS CITED ABOVE

3. The only requirement for membership in CoDA is a desire for healthy and loving relationships.

4. Each group should remain autonomous except in matters affecting other groups or CoDA as a whole.

5. Each group has but one primary purpose--to carry its message to other co-dependents who still suffer.

6. A CoDA gruop ought never endorse, finance or lend the CoDA name to any related facility or outside enterprise. lest problems of money, property and prestige divert us from our primary spiritual aim.

7. Every CoDA group ought to be fully self-supporting declining outside contributions.

8. Co-dependents Anonymous should remain forever non-professional, but our service centers may employ special workers.

9. CoDA, as such, ought never be organised; but we may create service boards or committees directly responsible to those they serve.

10. CoDA has no opinion on outside issues; hence the CoDA name ought never be drawn into public controversy.

11. Our public relations policy is based on attraction rather than promotion; we need always maintain personal anonymity at the level of press, radio and films.

12. Anonymity is the spiritual foundation of all our traditions; ever reminding us to place principles before personalities.

(d) The leader usually repeats a practical working rule of CoDA meetings that there is no "cross-talk", whether in the form of encouraging "feedback" or suggestions, advice or criticism. This principle is simply an implication of recovery from Codependency. To be free from all habits of control and compliance, each person has the right to work with their own understanding and at their own

DAY EIGHT : FOLLOWING

pace. The prohibition against cross-talk helps create an atmosphere of freedom. The reason for this is evident. From the respectful listening and silence of the group everyone comes to know that, whatever they may say and however they may say it, they need not fear being censored by comments or criticism, nor need they strive for approval from anyone.

(e) In keeping with the seventh tradition a small box or basket is passed around for participants to donate freely whatever they wish to give in order to help support the local group with its incidental expenses--rent for the meeting room, postage for correspondence, etc.

(f) Either at this time or at the very end of the meeting any "business" or announcements are dealt with-- e.g. change of venue, or time of meetings, advance news of a special meeting or event on the CoDA calendar, etc.

(g) The heart of every regular weekly CoDA meeting is personal sharing. Members are free to speak or not. If someone does not feel comfortable sharing, they simply say, "I pass." If the group is made up of fifteen people or more, smaller groups are now made by randomly counting off -- 2, 1-2, etc. All the ones go to one location, the twos to another. A veteran member volunteers or is designated to animate the group. Smaller groups of seven to ten persons allow everyone 3-5 minutes to share their personal experience of Codependency over the past week. The topic of sharing typically is how each person has lived one of the twelve steps of the CoDA programme. Some groups decide to spend one month (therefore, four weekly meetings) on one each of the 12 Steps. The focus of participants is themselves, demonstrating responsibility for their own recovery. So the first person personal pronoun "I" is encouraged rather than the generic, editorial "we". Members usually will share ups and downs of the past week in their struggle to live out one of the 12 Steps. Working on the principle that experience is valuable if reflected upon, even "defeats" over the past week can be turned into "victories" by making them good educational experiences--learning from mistakes. Another relevant topic of sharing is for each person to describe how they heard about CoDA, how they realised that they are codependents, how they are doing in recognising their own codependent patterns of thinking, feeling and behaving, how the promises of CoDA recovery are being realised in their lives. Since for many codependents sharing in public does not come easily due to feelings of fear, shame, and guilt, initial sharings are simple and brief. Confidentiality is a principle which every animator will repeat: "WHAT YOU HEAR HERE/WHAT YOU SEE HERE/ WHEN YOU LEAVE HERE/ THEN LEAVE IT HERE!" The rule against cross-talk is another encouragement. No criticism, no comments, no evaluations. Careful, attentive, concerned listening by all the members is a great incentive to speakers. Everything is important if it's coming from someone's life and painful experience.

(h) The full group comes together before adjourning--regularly a meeting is of 60-90 minutes. Final announcements are made and then the Lord's Prayer is offered together. Sometimes, if this is culturally acceptable, members join hands during the final prayer in order to express solidarity with everyone in the room. The final note is an encouraging theme which everyone says together: "KEEP COMING BACK; IT WORKS--IF YOU WORK AT IT!"

Why CoDA Succeeds In Fostering Commitment

Before summing up, a final remark about CoDA's system of Sponsorship. From the experience of all 12 Step recovery programmes, the best, surest way for an individual to succeed is with a SPONSOR. This is a guide whom each codependent chooses for themselves to help them faithfully "work" through the Twelve Step Programme. A sponsor is, therefore, a kind of role- model, an example of commitment, someone who understands the programme and who is working at it successfully. Sponsors share with the person they sponsor experiences and discoveries from their own struggles with Codependency. They listen carefully, respecting the unique pace of the other; sponsors also are ex-

DAY EIGHT : FOLLOWING

emplary at keeping confidences. When needed, they also are able to confront others with the truth-in-love. They do not play the therapist, nor do they give advice or indulge in "fixing" or "rescuing". They do not abuse the relationship for selfish ends--professionally, sexually or personally. Sponsors are people who "walk like they talk". They are not teachers but fellow pilgrims and faithful witnesses to CoDA's principles and promises: discovery, recovery and selfrespect.

God's Spirit has in periods of special stress and crisis inspired so many founders and foundresses of religious orders down through the centuries in order to bring succour and relief to suffering humanity. In this same pattern, I do not have any doubt that the Lord also inspired the Twelve Step recovery programme. Without substituting religion, it is basically religious and wholly sound in its principles. I have heard that the people who are most committed to the Twelve Step way of life are committed christians. I believe this. And I think that this is where IHR participants can learn a very important dimension of healing from CoDA and other groups following similar programmes based upon the 12 Steps. I summarise some of these important learnings which are very relevant to Day Eight's theme of faithful following the Way and the Truth:

(1) Healing most of the time means walking a <u>life-long road of recovery.</u> Especially when the matter is inner healing, achieving wholeness and holiness demands constant effort and faithful commitment to a proven programme, a regimen of spiritual, mental, emotional health.

(2) No one is healed alone, by themselves, isolated from society. Healing and recovery take place within a therapeutic community of people who are themselves "wounded healers". We need regular contact--weekly--biweekly--with this community for support and guidance. This is the way God made us and this is the only way we can flourish in health and holiness. Our full potential can be reached only within a community and in mutual service to this community.

A TIME FOR HEALING

*HOLY HOUR: The participants are encouraged to spend this hour with their Eucharistic Lord humbly asking Him to give them the grace of faithful commitment to Him, to follow always His truth and love, to the guidance of the Holy Spirit, to open, encouraging fellowship.

* EUCHARISTIC CELEBRATION: Suggested readings for today's theme are: 1) Jos 24: 1-2, 14-16, 19-24; 2) Ps 1, response from Jr 21:8, "Look, I offer you a choice between the way of life and the way of death"; 3) Lk 9:23-25 or 9:57-62.

* NIGHT COMMON SHARING: The animator suggests that the sharing of each person focus on what they have decided in-the-Lord by way of commiting themselves to keeping alive and deepening within their lives a spirit of on-going inner healing. A final prayer may be offered by the main animator that the participants would now go forth and share their healing experiences with others. In this way each retreatant will become a missionary of wholeness and holiness.

* TEAM EVALUATION: Since this is the final day, the team may choose to dispense with the meeting or else spend it as a time of thanking God for all graces within the IHR.

DAY EIGHT : FOLLOWING

PRAYER FOR THE GRACE TO FOLLOW
(For Day Eight)

Abba, unimaginably tender, incorruptly faithful Father mine/
Jesus Word eternally You sent to me as Mary's Boy, my Brother/
Broken body crushed upon a cross I gave Him back to You a corpse/
Glorified alive fore'er, You raised Him up returned to be my Lord/
Can I now say: No! I refuse to follow Your faithful Son, my God/
Wise Lover, calling me to pledge myself, walking with Him, my life/

Jesus, Friend Unchanging, promise once again to be by me/
Down the road behind at ev'ry turn You've proven true/
Each morn, Lord, You beckoned me once more to follow Your lead/
Whose word can I trust, whose hand take, whose way go, if not Yours/

Spirit, cowards turned into heroines and heroes on Pentecost Day/
Confident, ennobled, eloquent, unlearned fisherfolk went forth/
Spreading God's Goodnews for kings and paupers, simply everyone/
Melt me, Advocate, mold and heal me firm to follow Jesus as they/

APPENDIX A

NOTES FOR OPTIONAL DAYS NINE & TEN

Inner Healing Retreats are of various lengths, according to the amount of time available to those making them. Some can afford only five days, others eight, others ten. Considering everything, I have found that ten days is about ideal. The most important reasons for this are two: (1) evangelisation and conversion of hearts and minds may not be rushed. (2) The heart of an IHR is healing of memories for broken, wounded relationships, many of which go back to early childhood. This process is painful and it is time-consuming. People may not be hurried through this. In my experience ten days is about average for most retreatants to experience conversion and inner healing. For a certain percentage ten days are not sufficient; the extra time must be sought either in another IHR or else in personal spiritual direction.

DAY NINE: A Time For Healing By Reaching Out

* **THEME:** REACHING OUT in mission to those in need.

* **AIM OF THE DAY:** (a) to realise that Christ's Holy Spirit through the dynamic of faith-maturation moves the christian community to move out compassionately to all other peoples for their healing and salvation; (b) to understand that the gift of physical healing is a continuation of Christ's ministry which He gave to His Church in order to confirm the proclamation of God's Goodnews with signs and wonders; (c) to experience how practically the witness of christian healing works.

* **MORNING PRAYER:** Ps. 117 *("Alleluia! Praise Yahweh, all nations......")*. This is the shortest psalm but extremely rich. It calls all peoples to praise God because of His strong, constant love. This faithful love has been revealed perfectly forever in Jesus Christ, who as the Wounded Healer offers integral healing to a humanity ravaged by sin and death. The message of Ps. 117 is very much

APPENDIX A

needed today in India, especially by Christ's disciples who are sent by His Spirit to help both christians and followers of all religions realise that as a country we can survive and flourish only in mutual love and collaboration.

* MEDITATION: Mk 16:14-20 is the great missionary mandate from the Risen Lord Jesus to His Pilgrim, Missionary Church. The animator does well to point out that the prophetic church's words can and must be corroborated by healing done as a loving service in the name of Jesus (see verses 17-18). These wonders witness to everyone, even to those without faith, that Jesus is alive and active within His apostles, He *"the Lord working with them and confirming the word by the signs that accompanied it."*

* COMMON REFLECTIONS I-III: The points for reflection today locate the ministry of healing the overall mission of Christ and His Church. Both MISSION and HEALING are rich themes biblically, liturgically and pastorally. The heart of today's theme of REACHING OUT is in a theology of COMMUNION. This cannot be overstressed. By God's calling the Church in its every member is in communion with the Most Holy Trinity. The Father has sent His Only Son on a mission of universal redemption. The Father and Son have sent the Spirit on a mission of universal sanctification. The Spirit anoints, consecrates, seals and sends the Church in her members through baptism, confirmation, charisms and continual guidance through the Church's ministries of teaching, preaching and governing.

Today we wish to give attention to the Church's mission of physical healing. For this reason we now present some principles of the christian healing ministry.

Wounded World And Wounded Healers

* ALL PEOPLE ARE IN NEED OF CONSTANT HEALING: We are not spectators but participants in a pilgrimage towards wholeness and holiness. All of us are broken, wounded, unwhole. Each person is a pilgrim called by the Lord Jesus Himself to intergral healing.

A TIME FOR HEALING

* **WE ARE MORTAL BUT WE ARE ALSO BORN INTO LIFE OF FULLNESS FOREVER:** The bad news is that, being members of a sinful family, we are all without exception destined to die once physically. The good news is that we are baptised into a life of integral wholeness and fullness of life forever. This fullness will be ours in "Life after life". Sickness and death were not in God's plan for His children. These came on earth as the bitter fruits of original sin. Sickness and death remain grim realities, even after Christ's redemption, as reminders to us that the satanic option of rebellion against God naturally leads to eternal death. But Jesus has radically redeemed us and made us whole. Therefore, sickness of any kind and death are to be resisted appropriately, so that we can get on with the purpose of our christian lives, the fulfilment of our mission: to do God's will for us in every circumstance of our lives.

* **THE LORD WANTS US WELL:** We are called to be well--healthy enough to fulfill our unique missions. Each of us is sent to achieve some task/s for preparing for the Reign of God. This mission is the purpose for which God created us and sent us into the world: to contribute towards Christ's Kingdom of truth, love, justice and communion of all peoples. Jesus came among us as a Wounded Healer, vulnerable, weak, mortal. We, too, are in Him Wounded Healers, relying wholly upon Him, recognising and accepting our own weaknesses. This is why Paul the Apostle could say with real joy: *"It is, then, about my weaknesses that I am happiest of all to boast, so that the power of Christ may rest upon me; and that is why I am glad of weaknesses, insults, constraints, persecutions and distress for Christ's sake. For it is when I am weak that I am strong."* (2 Co 12:9-10)

* **EVERY FAITHFUL PRAYER FOR HEALING IS ANSWERED:** We may not, do not and cannot control the process of integral healing. The Lord alone knows what is best. *"For the heavens are as high above earth as my ways are above your ways, my thoughts above your thoughts."* (Is 55:9) What does this Word of God mean practically, when we, as Christ's envoys, pray for healing? (1) We may petition God for a *physical* healing, but Christ can choose a

APPENDIX A

more needed area of healing--e.g. on the *emotional* or *spiritual* level. (2) We may want a TOTAL cure here and now, Christ the Healer in His infinite wisdom may decide that a gradual, slower PROCESS OF HEALING over a longer period of time is much better for all concerned. (3) We humans do not heal; GOD ALONE HEALS through Christ in the Spirit. We are called on to collaborate as servants, as partners. Medicine or surgery may be part of this needed collaboration, but in the end, it is the Lord who heals. So, we keep our eyes on the Lord always. (4) Healing is an act of CHRISTIAN LOVING. Jesus commands us to love as He has loved us. In the ministry of healing the most important dimension is that of *"soaking the patient in Christ's love"*. (5) We may assume that authentic healing is total and permanent. But it may also be PARTIAL AND TEMPORARY. As such it is not less a grace, no less a healing from the Lord. (6) We may rightly proclaim that Jesus the Lord is the Healer, and then conclude wrongly that our attitudes and actions really don't matter for effective healing. But, in point of proven fact *out attitudes, both those of the patients and of those ministering to them, are very important.* Some common blocks to healing: (a) consciously or unconsciously, patients may not actually want to be healed; (b) knowingly or unknowingly, patients may be holding grudges, unforgivingness, resentment, anger and hatred towards people living around them--like parents, brothers/sisters, spouse, etc. Patients perceive that someone has hurt them deeply and the memories of these hurts are still present, perhaps many years later. Such "wounded" memories from the past can be the root causes of present sicknesses.

* JESUS HEALS NOT AS A MARKETPLACE DOCTOR BUT AS LORD AND SAVIOUR: As Christ's friends and missioners of healing we may not cheapen His healing presence but failing to invite patients to make an act of faith in Him as Lord. Jesus is not like some bazaar healer who comes only when needed to relieve pain. Christ is not a mercenary but the all-loving, sovereign Lord of life.

Getting To The Heart Of Healing: A Reconciled Spirit

Before healing is attempted both patients and those praying with them need to have reconciled hearts towards all peoples. This means they must give and receive unconditional forgiveness to those with whom they may not yet be reconciled. *"I mean, God was in Christ reconciling the world to Himself not holding anyone's faults against them, but entrusting to us the message of reconciliation. So we are ambassadors for Christ . . . and in the name of Christ we appeal to you to be reconciled to God. For our sake He made the sinless one a victim for sin, so that in Him we might become the uprightness of God . . .now is the real time of favour, now the day of salvation is here."* (2 Co 5:19-21, 6:1-2)

Physical Ills From Wounded Feelings

In my earlier book, *Hidden Springs To Healing,* I have presented a chart which lists some of the common ailments afflicting us in different parts of our bodies, top to toe. Alongside these ills I have indicated in another column some root causes that often produce illness which are called psychosomatic. *Psycho* (mental- emotional) + *somatic* (bodily) illnesses are those physical disorders caused or influenced by our state of mind and emotions. Some reliable experts estimate that as many as 90% or more of our sicknesses are at root psychosomatic. For example, a common ailment is pain in the legs or feet. Physical examinations of this distressing disorder may lead to no clear diagnosis. If the patient is asked the following questions, however, the main cause for this pain in the lower extremities may be discovered. (1) How long has this pain been there? (2) Just before the perceived onset of pain was there any situation which caused tension or anxiety? (3) If so, has this anxiety been resolved? Typical responses to the above questions are that there was instability or insecurity just before the pain began and that no, these were not resolved but are still present. Coming to grips with the root cause of this pain, namely, the anxiety and tensions, brings relief. Six areas of the body are listed here together

APPENDIX A

with common bodily disorders associated with each area and in capital letters some emotional root causes.

Area I (head, eyes, ears, sinus):
RESENTMENT, UNFORGIVINGNESS, GUILT, DOUBT, FEAR, ANXIETY.

Area II (nose, mouth, throat, neck, shoulders, upper back):
HOSTILITY, NEGATIVITY, HOLDING BACK, FEELINGS OF REJECTION.

Area III (chest, lungs, heart--blood pressure, etc.) :
ANGER, ENVY, DESPAIR, UNACCEPTANCE, DISCOURAGEMENT, INFERIORITY, FEAR, INSENSITIVITY, ENMITY.

Area IV (stomach, intestines, lower back):
GRIEF, SORROW, SUPPRESSED FEARS, DENIAL OF UNFORGIVINGNESS.

Area V (reproductive system) :
UNRESOLVED SEXUAL TENSIONS.

Area VI (legs, knees, feet):
ANXIETIES, INSECURITY, INSTABILITY.

Praying For Physical Healing

About twenty-five percent of gospel accounts describe Jesus healing some form of human pain and sickness--skin disorders, deafness, blindness, muteness, paralysis, diabolic obsession and possession, death itself. Jesus dealt with patients with deep respect, freedom and love. He asked them what they wanted and whether they desired to be healed. He laid His hands upon them lovingly and ordered the sickness to depart. As envoys of Jesus we want to imitate our Lord, because our effectiveness lies in one fact alone: we continue His mission of redemptive love in the power of Christ's Holy Spirit. Therefore, the following steps seem to me to be essential:

A TIME FOR HEALING

(1) Enquire of the patient what THEY THEMSELVES DESIRE.

(2) Ask about how long the disorder has existed and whether there is need of reconciliation. If so, proceed with this first, BEFORE praying for physical healing.

(3) Imagine our Lord Himself present--invisibly He is! Invoke His presence by quietly praying in a voice which the patient can hear. If appropriate, place hand/s gently on the patient's head or affected area. Holy articles are recommended for use: blessed oil and salt, holy water, a crucifix or rosary. Being sacramentals, they help centre the prayerful attention of all on Christ the Healer and on His Paschal Victory over all evil.

(4) "Soak" the patient in God's love. This may be done by remembering God's graciousness for this person in his/her salvation history, recalling the great graces already received: a) creation through God the Father, b) redemption through Jesus Saviour, c) sanctification through the Spirit Advocate. Other graces, which are special to this person, may also be recalled. Above all, christian healers proclaim God's glory plan for this person's total healing in Christ.

(5) We humbly submit our petition for physical gifts on condition that such healing be according to God's eternal glory plan of love and fullness of life for this patient. If physical healing here and now is according to that plan, we claim it respectfully in Christ's name. In other words, *we do not order God but we ask trustfully*, as befits beloved children of an all-loving Father. We may publicly admit that we do not know whether such physical healing is for this person's total good and according to the person's mission. What we do know is that God loves this person infinitely and that God has decreed total healing for him/her in Christ for eternity.

(6) After praying a while--five or ten minutes--we may ask the patient how they are, whether they experience anything. Discernment is done whether to continue praying, or to schedule another prayer session later, or to counsel the patient to continue privately praising and thanking God.

APPENDIX A

* HOLY HOUR: A session for physical healing may be conducted within the Holy Hour with Blessed Sacrament exposed. In this way focus of attention is centred easily on Jesus. Everyone who desires to be prayed over is given a chance, if after a set period of prayer sitting patients interchange chairs with those who prayed for them. It helps if the animator stirs up faith in Christ's healing presence in the Eucharist. To this end I recommend two books to retreatants, which deal with Our Lord's continuing healing presence through His Sacraments, particularly in the Eucharist. These are: *Healing Through The Sacraments* by Michael March, O.P. and *Healing Through The Mass* by Robt. Degrandis, S.S.J.

* EUCHARISTIC CELEBRATION: Readings are: 1) Jm 5:13-17 or Ac 5:12-16; 2) Ps. 46 or 88; 3) Mt 9:35-37. A Votive Mass of the Most Holy Eucharist may be used, together with the Second Prayer For Reconciliation.

DAY TEN: A Time For Healing By Growing

*THEME: GROWING in the Lord by living more and more obedient to His Spirit.

* AIM OF THE DAY: (a) To realise that by God's wonderful plan from all eternity we are called through Christ to be open for growth unto fullness. That this may be our permanent attitude, our faith needs to become universal, embracing not only all peoples but all creation; (b) to appreciate more deeply our vocations to live in communion with Christ, to continue His mission by becoming who we are already in the Father's heart; (c) to commit ourselves to life-in-the-Spirit, being open and obedient to God's plan for building up the Body of Christ through the transformation of ourselves and our world, our deepest aspiration being *"Thy Kingdom come!"*

* MORNING PRAYER: Ps. 150 ("Alleluia! Praise God in His holy place......"). *The IHR concludes with a day of communion in-the-Spirit with the whole of creation, through praise, thanks and trustful openness.*

A TIME FOR HEALING

* MEDITATION: Scriptural texts today will focus on growth into the fullness of Christ by mature collaboration with His Spirit. E.g. Jn 1:1-18; 1 Jn 3:1-2; Col 1:15-20; 2:9-13; Ep 3:14-21; 4:1- 13.

* COMMON REFLECTIONS I-III: The animator wishes to help retreatants consolidate the graces which God has given them during this IHR by realising that gifts of healing are for promoting only personal holiness but holiness of Christ's Body and the world's salvation. Vatican II's *Dogmatic Constitution On The Church,* chapter 8. "The Call To Holiness" and the *Pastoral Constitution On The Church In The Modern World",* Part I, Chapter III, "On Human Activity In The Universe" offer plenty of solid reflections for the day's theme. This teaching can be harmonised with related biblical themes, such as *growth. fullness, life-in- the-Spirit, pilgrimage and mission.*

* HOLY HOUR: A quiet, grateful review of graces given to each person is recommended. It is a time of "counting our blessings". Retreatants are encouraged to express their gratitude to God and to pledge themselves anew to use these divine gifts in His service. Fidelity to our christian vocation means growth in faith-unto-fullness. It also implies that christians promote spiritual growth in others--not just Christians and those of religions also. through ecumenism, inter- religious dialogue and collaboration for a more just Indian society.

* EUCHARISTIC CELEBRATIONS: Readings are taken either from among those given in today's meditation or the designated texts for Pentecost's Vigil (or, for the Solemnity itself). The Proper may be taken from a votive Mass of the Holy Spirit along with the Fourth Eucharistic Prayer.

APPENDIX B

THE JOHARI WINDOW : HELP FOR COMMUNICATION

From its name the "Johari Window" mentioned early in our text seems to be of Indian origin. Actually, it is a concept from two American Behavioural Scientists whose first names are Joe and Harry! This instrument is simple and effective to understand what are the essential ingredients for good communication between an individual and her/his community. Below I present the Johari Window in a simplified, adapted form to promote easier understanding by my Indian readers.

THE INDIVIDUAL

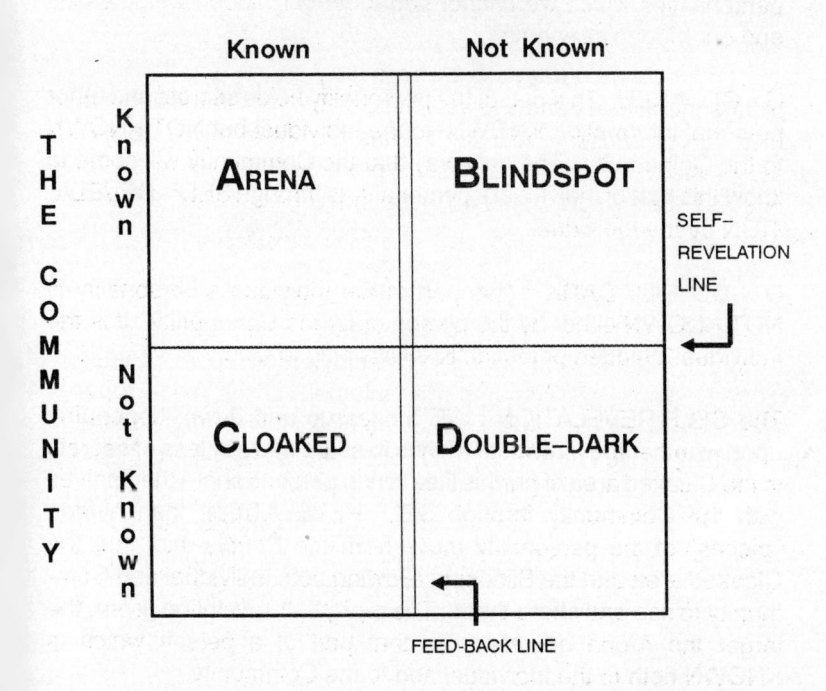

	Known	Not Known
Known	ARENA	BLINDSPOT
Not Known	CLOAKED	DOUBLE–DARK

(Rows labeled: THE COMMUNITY)

SELF–REVELATION LINE

FEED-BACK LINE

Explanation Of The Concept

A = ARENA. This is that part of the individual's personality which is KNOWN both to the person and to the Community in which she/he lives. The larger the Arena, the more transparent the person.

B = BLINDSPOT. This is NOT KNOWN to the Individual but it is KNOWN to the Community. The only way the Individual can become aware of this part of her/his personality is by FEED-BACK from the Community. The term "BLINDSPOT" comes from an analogy with a person's range of eyesight. Physically people cannot see what is behind them. For instance, to know whether the back of the clothing we are wearing is in proper order or not, we must rely on others to tell us. In the same way psychologically, we all need a Community to inform us about that part of our own personalities which we cannot see--both our hidden weaknesses and our hidden strengths.

C = CLOAKED. This part of the personality holds secrets and other personal information KNOWN to the Individual but NOT KNOWN to the Community. The only way that the Community will come to know this part of Individual's personality is through SELF- REVELATION by the Individual.

D = DOUBLE-DARK. This part of the Individual's personality is NOT KNOWN either by the person or by the Community. It is the Individual's hidden potential, KNOWN only to God.

The SELF-REVELATION LINE moves up and down, depending upon whether the Individual wishes to share more or less of secrets in the Cloaked area of her/his life. When persons share themselves with the Community through SELF-REVELATION, then hidden "pieces" of the personality move from the Double-dark into the Cloaked area and the Blindspot allowing both Individual and Community to see and share them. The more Self-revelation given, the larger the Arena becomes, i.e that part of a person which is KNOWN both to the Individual and to the Community.

APPENDIX B

The FEED-BACK LINE moves left to right, depending upon whether the Community wishes to share with Individuals that part of their personalities which is Not Known to them but is Known by the Community. The more Feed-back given, the larger the Arena becomes. Having explained the dynamics of this concept of communication, we are now ready to look at different kinds of personality "windows". If the Johari is calibrated with numbers, e.g. 0-50, for both Self-Revelation (SR) and Feed-back (FB), then the readings can be more easily communcated. A "Talker" would be described as SR 40/FB 10; a "Listener" as SR 10/FB 40, etc.

(1) THE EXTROVERTED TALKER: For example, an Individual who likes to tell people about her/himself scores high on the SR scale with 40 (or more) but low on the FB scale with only 10 (or less). This means such extroverted persons will have a big Blindspot, because they either do not want Feedback from the Community or else for whatever reason they do not get it. The Talker's Johari Window looks like this:

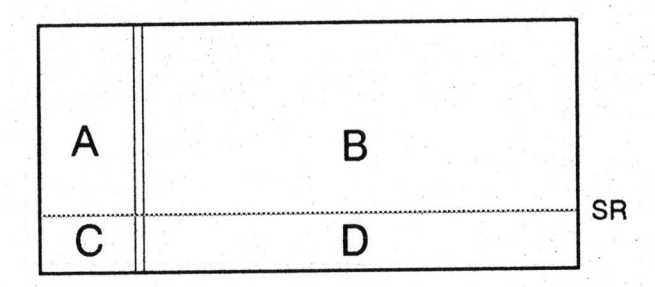

A	B
C	D

SR

(2) THE INTROVERTED LISTENER: The opposite situation exists for Individuals who seek Feed-back from the Community, but once they get it, they do not share their own thoughts and feelings. Such an introverted personality may score 40 (or more) on the FB scale but only 10 (or less) on the SR scale. Introverted listeners will be virtually unknown to the Community in which they live. Their Cloaked area will be very large, as is shown below:

```
+----------------+--+
|        A       |B | SR
|················|··|
|        C       |D |
+----------------+--+
```

(3) THE TRANSPARENT PERSONALITY: According to the Johari Window an ideal Individual in Community is a person who not only shares themselves but also seeks--and--gets--accurate feedback. Both their SR and FB ratings may be 40 or above. They are called "transparent" personalities. They will be using more and more of their God-given potential because they make their true selves known and they rely interdependently upon their Communities for regular, healthy feedback. Their Johari looks like this:

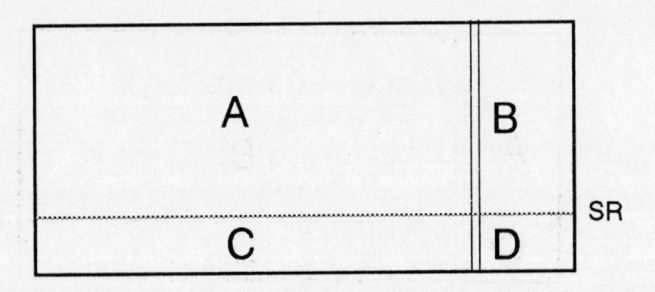

```
+----------------+--+
|                |  |
|        A       |B |
|                |  |
|················|··| SR
|        C       |D |
+----------------+--+
```

APPENDIX C

CATCHING DREAMS

Dreams and their true interpretation have been important to all peoples of all cultures throughout human history. Both Old Testament and New Testament books indicate that God has used dreams to gift people in various ways: giving vital information, timely warnings or encouragement in midst of serious crises. In the past several decades much research by behavioural scientists has been done, which takes interpretation of dreams out of the confines of psychiatry and makes it available to ordinary people. A most readable and enlightening paperback on this subject, which I recommend to IHR participants, is that of Dr. Ann Faraday entitled *Dream Power*. What Faraday presents seems to me most useful for helping retreatants learn both how to "catch" dreams and how to understand them for personal growth. Much of what I present below relies on Faraday's study together with some of my own reflections.

What Is A Dream?

St. Augustine writes that if you asked him, "What is meaning of Time?", he would say that he knows; but asked to define Time, he is perplexed how to do it. The same is true about dreams. From personal experience everyone knows what dreams are. However, pressed for a description, there are very few answers. Dream expert Calvin Hall gives this definition, which fits aptly for at least our longer dreams:

"A dream is a succession of images, predominantly visual in quality, which are experienced during sleep. A dream commonly has one or more scenes, several characters in addition to the dreamer, and a sequence of actions and interactions usually involving the dreamer. It resembles a motion picture or dramatic production in which the dreamer is both a participant and an observer. Although a dream is a hallucination, since the events of a dream do not actually take place, the dreamer experiences it as though he were seeing something real."

Professor Hall gives four main rules for dreams interpretation:

(1) DREAMS ARE NOT REPRESENTATIONS OF OBJECTIVE REALITY BUT REALITY AS IT APPEARS TO THE DREAMER. In other words, the dreamer, like an artist, depicts a vision of reality as he/she sees it.

(2) EVERYTHING IN THE DREAM IS TRACEABLE TO THE DREAMER. Whatsoever the contents of the dream, they come from the dreamer.

(3) DREAMS PORTRAY THE DREAMER'S ALTERNATIVE VIEWS OF SELF, OTHERS AND HER/HIS LIFE-SITUATION. All people have uncouscious judgments about themselves, people around them and the world. Some of these "other" conceptions about reality are hidden from awareness; they are in the unconscious. They can and do bubble up to the surface of our consciousness in dreams, where they are dramatised in symbolic language.

(4) DREAMS ARE BEST INTERPRETED IN PATTERNS AND SERIES RATHER THAN SINGLY OR SEPARATELY. The contents of dreams come from us, the dreamers, who give them continuity and meaning. Dreams, therefore, should be understood in this wider context, according to our own life-experience. In other words, we can make sense of our dreams' figurative language by examining them in the light of our own life-circumstances and life-histories.

What Are Dreams About And How Do They Work?

An important aspect of dreams lies in their power to show us that we have perceived reality at much greater depth than we had imagined. Before dreaming, these intuitions were experiences that

APPENDIX C

we had perceived; our minds had instantaneously recorded them and then filed them away in our unconscious for future reference. When we dream, this precious material becomes conscious, making it available to be used. Dream contents show us other dimensions of how we understand: (a) ourselves, (b) our relationships with significant other people, (c) our actual life-situations, (d) our impulses and urges, and (e) our conflicts.

Summing up some of the main ways dreams can be beneficial to us: (1) They can REMIND us of important facts. (2) They can creatively SHOW US HOW TO DO AND SAY THINGS about which we are concerned. (3) They can WARN us of real dangers. (4) They can INTUIT the truth of people and situations, helping us become aware of certain dimensions about which we were not yet conscious. They do this in the following ways:

* A dream uses SYMBOLIC PICTURE LANGUAGE REVEALING to the dreamer how she/he understands persons and circumstances unconsciously.

* The dream's time-frame is THE PRESENT but incorporating significant experiences of the past. The dream's message is FOR TODAY.

* Dream interpretation comes from the dreamer asking her/himself, "GIVEN MY OWN EXPERIENCE, WHAT USEFUL MESSAGE DO I GET FROM THIS DREAM'S SYMBOLIC LANGUAGE?"

The meaning of dreams, in other words, is not to be left to highly trained psychiatrists. Dream interpretation can be very helpful for solving everyday life-problems. Dreams can offer penetrating insights towards a better, more realistic understanding of ourselves, our lives, and our activities. If sometimes disturbing elements show themselves in dreams--e.g. situations that evoke much fear, anxiety, terror, disordered desires--we can thank God for calling our attention to these emotions through the dream and then consciously we can offer them to the Lord for healing. What human sciences offer us by way of "natural" explanation, in no way excludes the

A TIME FOR HEALING

possibility of God's graces coming to us through dreams. For this dimension, I suggest, as a beginning, Leon-Dufour's short article, "Dreams", in his *Dictionary Of Biblical Theology.*

How To Catch A Dream

Dr. Faraday suggests some very practical ways of "catching" dreams, that is, a technique for remembering and recording them for use. Here in summary is her twelve step method:

(1) Before going to sleep at night, make sure there is something WRITING MATERIAL near your bed.

(2) Keep a FLASHLIGHT or bedlight for ready use also.

(3) Tell yourself that you will: a) dream, b) awaken and c) write it down. This POSITIVE SUGGESTION is important--and effective.

(4) If you are a deep sleeper, set an ALARM CLOCK to go off-- softly, please!--about two hours after you normally fall asleep. After you have recorded the first dream, set the clock again for another two hour period. In this way will be able to catch more than one dream in a single night. An option to this every-two-hour routine is to set the alarm for a little before your routine rising time.

(5) When you awake from your dream, with eyes still closed QUIETLY AND GENTLY review it in your mind. Then slowly sit up, and turn on a light. Like when you have a fish on your line, any sudden movement upon awakening are dangerous. If you're not careful, you can lose it.

(6) At once jot down your dream IN DETAIL.

(7) Record your FEELINGS too that accompany the dream during or after it. Also write down what you think the dream means-- e.g. in the context of your previous day's happenings. This "first information report" is important for later interpretation.